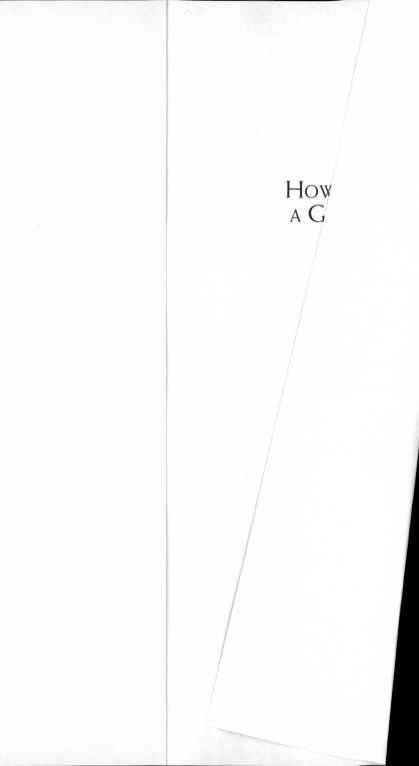

How
A G

How to Raise a Gentleman

Kay West

Rutledge Hill Press®
Nashville, Tennessee

A Division of Thomas Nelson, Inc.
www.ThomasNelson.com

For my parents, who taught me manners;
For my children, who taught me parenting;
And to RRT, for the rest

Published by Rutledge Hill Press, a Division of Thomas Nelson, Inc.,
P.O. Box 141000, Nashville, Tennessee 37214.

Library of Congress Cataloging-in-Publication Data
West, Kay, 1955–
    How to raise a gentleman / Kay West.
        p. cm.
    ISBN 1-55853-940-9 (hardcover)
    ISBN 1-40160-087-5 (leather edition)
    1. Child rearing. 2. Etiquette for children and teenagers. 3. Etiquette for
boys. I. Title.
    HQ769 .W446 2001
    649'.132—dc21

2001004338

Printed in the United States of America
05 06 — 12 11 10 9 8 7

CONTENTS

INTRODUCTION

It is every parent's mission to provide his or her children with what they need to thrive and succeed—socially, academically, and professionally. Today, there are many tools and media with which to attain this goal. Some parents employ rather extreme measures, such as pre-enrolling their not-yet-conceived children in acclaimed nurseries or strapping headphones on the expectant mother's belly so that the dozing fetus might cultivate an *in utero* interest in opera, foreign language, or the stock market.

Infants are thrust into early educational development with all sorts of visual, aural, and tactile stimuli: toddlers are enrolled in enrichment classes and group sports, kindergartners tackle the rudiments of algebra, and second-graders stay after school for technology, Spanish, or soccer clubs.

Parents scrutinize their son's every movement for signs that he might be "gifted" in some field; if his crayoned scribble-scrabble suggests a clearly superior understanding of proportion and perspective, he is placed in an art class or under the dedicated care of a trained professional with high hopes of developing his budding talent. Such nurturing could one day lead to acceptance at a prestigious institute of higher education, an astounding offer by a professional sports team, or a meteoric rise in a technology firm. This is all well and good, but in the drive to propel our children to ever-higher stratospheres of achievement what can fall by the wayside are invaluable lessons in good manners, common courtesy, and a familiarity with the most useful rules of etiquette.

Good manners are not nearly as complicated as fractions, as repetitive as scales, or as physically taxing as throwing a breaking fastball. And though your son may be gifted at mathematics, music, or sports, good manners are not something he is born with.

Young gentlemen spring forth from any well; blue-blooded breeding does not always lead to blue-ribbon manners. Princes-in-waiting may be more accustomed to fine dining than boys raised on a pig farm, but familiarity with place settings and the proper use of forks is less valuable than kindness and the proper use of "please" and "thank you."

Good manners begin and end with common courtesy. While matters of proper etiquette fill weighty volumes defining a formal code of behavior, common courtesy is much simpler. What is courtesy but conducting oneself with a respect for others and the world we inhabit? It is based on civility, kindness, and consideration. It is being mindful of others, whether you are in their presence or in the presence of their home and possessions. It makes other people feel good about themselves and about you. In short, common courtesy and its natural progeny, good manners, are the embodiment of the Golden Rule: Do unto others as you would have them do unto you.

Courtesy and good manners begin with the assimilation of the examples set for a boy by his parents. *How To Raise A Gentleman* is a book for parents who want to do the right thing but may need a few pointers themselves. This is not a book of formal etiquette but a guide to good manners supported by a common sense collection of real-life advice, time-tested tips, and lessons learned. Ideally, this instruction manual will prove to be as helpful for parents as it is for sons.

Good manners will open more doors, charm more acquaintances, and make more memorable first impressions than all French, flute, and golf lessons combined. The basics can be acquired in toddlerhood and, with daily application, will last a lifetime. It is never too soon to begin or too late to catch up.

LEADING THE WAY TO GOOD MANNERS

26 Things to Remember

Use "please," "thank you,"
and "excuse me." Always.

———

Wait your turn.

———

Be generous with compliments
and stingy with criticism.

———

Listen to your child when he
speaks to you, even if you've
heard it before.

———

Do not discipline your child
in front of others.

———

Do not correct any child, other
than your own, on his manners,
and always do that privately.

———

Be clear about what you expect.

———

Be consistent.

———

Do not give in to temper tantrums.

———

Do not lose your temper.

———

Admit when you are wrong;
offer an apology when
you owe one.

———

Let your child know when
a discussion has become
a decision.

———

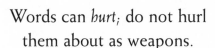

Words can *hurt;* do not hurl
them about as weapons.

———

Respect your child's privacy and
boundaries. Knock first.

———

Do not impose your ideology,
and respect those whose ideology
differs from your own.

———

Agree to disagree.

———

Give credit where
credit is due.

———

Hold the door.

———

Lend a hand.

———

Be a good sport.

———

Be a gracious loser and
a generous winner.

———

Give more than you are asked.

———

Don't take more than you need.

———

Leave a place cleaner
than you found it.

———

Do not respond to rudeness
with rudeness.

———

Winning is not the only thing,
and nice guys do finish first.

———

Chapter One

PLEASE, THANK YOU, EXCUSE ME, AND OTHER EARLY SOCIAL INTERVENTIONS

After "Mama" and "Papa," the very next word in your son's vocabulary will likely be "no." In the early stages using the word "no" typically does not indicate rudeness but a self-satisfied delight in finding a means to communicate displeasure other than crying, screaming, or squalling. It is also an easier word for tiny mouths to form than the more agreeable and pleasant "yes." As your boy's vocabulary expands, he will begin to communicate his wants and needs. This is the time to introduce the two magic words: "please" and "thank you."

As with most mannerly conduct, the best way to promote its practice is by example. Children want to emulate the adults in their lives and fit in with the rest of the family. If the words "please" and "thank you" are used without exception in your home, your budding young gentleman will follow suit. Using "please" and "thank you" yourself is also an opportunity to reward and promote other courteous behavior. "Thank you for using your fork instead of your fingers." "Please don't leave your shoes in the middle of the floor."

Except in the case of an emergency, encourage the use of the word "please" by never responding to a request unless and until the word is employed. Do not expect a three year old to deliver lengthy sentences such as "May I please have a cookie?" but help him see the difference between a request and a demand. "Cookie!" is a demand that grates on the nerves and will go unheeded. "Cookie, please" is a request so pleasing to the adult ear that it is likely to be met with the cheerful bestowal of the coveted item. (There are exceptions of course: cookies before meals is a no-no in my house, but I try to recognize the mannerly request by saying, "Because that was such a nice way to ask, it's hard to say no, but not before dinner. Maybe afterwards."

When your son's request is granted, he then responds by saying, "Thank you." Adults should, in turn, respond to this seminal display of civility with a modest expression of approval. A smile or quick hug is fine; rewards are not necessary for behavior that is eventually expected to be a matter of course, with the possible exception of potty training. In that taxing endeavor, the reward system is encouraged. Reserve your applause for accomplishments that deserve it, like straight As, a four-minute mile, or a full scholarship to Yale.

It is one small but impressive step from "please" and "thank you" to "yes, please" and "no, thank you," but one not to be expected until the child has mastered the former and uses them as habit. By then, "Would you like a cookie?" has two appropriate responses: "Yes, please" or "No, thank you."

The next phrase central to a young man's

socially correct lexicon is "Excuse me." The opportunities for its use will present themselves again and again:

If a young man inadvertently burps aloud or passes gas in the company of others, the minor offense will be easily forgiven if it is immediately followed by a polite "Excuse me."

A young gentleman never deliberately pushes or otherwise harms another person.

If a young man accidentally jostles another person or steps on toes, the appropriate way to make amends is simply by saying, "Excuse me."

A young gentleman does not interrupt adults when they are engaged in conversation—in person or on the telephone—but if the conversation is a lengthy one, and he has a pressing need that must be promptly attended to, then he might say, "Excuse me, Daddy. I really need to go to the bathroom now!" An attentive daddy will stop discussing last night's hockey game and attend to his son's request.

Should a young man need to have something repeated to him because it was unclear or he was unable to hear, he says, "Excuse me?" He does not say, "What?" or even worse, "Huh?"

You Know You Are Raising A Gentleman If . . .

He uses "please," "thank you," and "excuse me" on a consistent basis.

_____

He speaks when spoken to.

_____

He does not point out other children's lack of manners.

_____

When he doesn't understand something, he simply says, "Excuse me?" or "Would you repeat that?"

_____

He always knocks on a closed door,
particularly one that leads to a
bathroom or bedroom.

―――

He removes his cap when he sits down to
eat at a table in a home or restaurant.

PARENT POINTERS

Use "please," "thank you," and
"excuse me" in all encounters.

―――

Say "please" when making a
request of your son.

―――

Say "thank you" to your son after he
fulfills that request.

―――

Say "excuse me" if you must interrupt him,
even if it's a lengthy and seemingly endless
recounting of a Rug Rats movie.

―――

Knock on your son's bedroom or bathroom door before entering, unless there is a clear indication of danger.

_____

Occasionally note your son's developing sense of good manners.

_____

Compliment your son's friends on their good manners—but do not reprove them for a lack thereof. Pass along to other parents what lovely manners their sons have. There is nothing a parent likes to hear more about their son than, "Harry has such wonderful manners."

TRY THIS AT HOME

My sister is convinced that the moment a parent gets on the phone or goes into the bathroom there is an alarm that goes off, audible only to children, that inspires an immediate and pressing need for a parent's attention. My own experience has proven her correct. To discourage telephone interruptions from my son, I simply hold my hand up in front of his little face like a policeman stopping traffic or turn my back altogether. Unless it is an emergency, I do not stop my conversation until its natural conclusion. When in the bathroom, I lock the door to discourage walk-ins.

SOME GOOD ADVICE

When I was six years old and apparently quite smug about my superior manners, I pointed out to a friend lunching with me that she had not thanked my mother for her grilled cheese sandwich. My mother called me out to the kitchen and pointed out to me that by making my friend feel badly, I had exhibited far worse manners than she. Always remember that the core of good manners is not steadfast attendance to the rules of etiquette, but kindness, respect, and consideration for others.

Chapter Two

YES SIR, NO SIR, AND OTHER REGIONAL DIVIDES

People who live in the South often consider a Yankee's typical straightforwardness as discourteous. Conversely, many Yankees take a southerner's love for idle chit-chat with complete strangers as an unwelcome and extremely annoying intrusion. Without question there is a perception that Yankees are rude and southerners well-mannered. But having lived both north and south of the Mason-Dixon line, I have found plenty of examples of Yankee hospitality and southern chill.

Generally, southerners routinely embellish conversations with elaborate compliments, a practice Yankees consider a waste of time and phony baloney. When I first moved to the South, I was leaving a small market and heard

the proprietor say, "Come back!" I was stymied.
I knew I would never be in again, so I tried to
explain that I didn't live in the neighborhood
and probably wouldn't be back. The sales clerk
looked at me as if I were insane.

Nowhere are the cultural divides more obvious,
however, than in the use of "Sir" and "Ma'am."
There is one school of thought that believes
children should be taught to use the titles "Sir" and
"Ma'am" whenever they interact with an adult.
Young men who attend military academies will also
be expected to employ this form of address, and its
omission can be cause for severe punishment.

Otherwise, "Yes, Ma'am" and "No, Sir" are
forms of courtesy that are not frequently—if
ever—heard in the northeast or on the west
coast. In the South, however, and in parts of the
Midwest, such as Kansas and Oklahoma, they
are deep-rooted customs.

Growing up in the northeast, the only
opportunity I had to hear children my own age
use the words "Yes, Ma'am" and "No, Sir" was

when watching *The Waltons*. For the most part, life in the Waltons' home was harmonious. It would have been unthinkable for John-Boy to respond to his mother, Olivia, without saying "Yes, Ma'am " or "No, Ma'am."

When I moved to the South, I was amazed to find that this habit was not an affectation or television fabrication but a way of life for many families, though not taught or practiced as frequently or stringently as it once was.

Teaching your son to use "Sir" and "Ma'am" is a matter of personal taste, with some guidance necessary for its use. If you choose to require it from your son, do it consistently. It is confusing to require the titles for distant members of the family rarely seen but not for Uncle Ted who drops by the house once or twice a week or to use one practice for close friends of the family and another for professional acquaintances. It is not up to the child to assess the level of the relationship.

The measures for the usage of "Ma'am" and "Sir" are quite simple: age and status, with age being the primary consideration. As adults are always older than children, then "Sir" and "Ma'am" are used in conjunction with "Yes," "No," or "Excuse me" whenever your son speaks to an adult, including his parents. This is true even if your ten-year-old financial whiz kid has accumulated millions in the stock market and could buy and sell every adult in the room. They are still, by virtue of their years, his superior, and he should treat them accordingly.

For some adults the policy governing the use of "Ma'am" and "Sir" is not so grounded in tradition or formalities as it is a means to eliminate such grating responses as "Huh," "Yeah," or "Nah." If your son attends a school where proper deportment is a part of the curriculum, his teachers may require the use of "Sir" and "Ma'am" in the classroom. If that is inconsistent with your habits at home, the wishes of the teacher always take precedence in the classroom.

You Know You Are Raising A Gentleman If . . .

He routinely uses "Sir" and "Ma'am" if it is
a practice in your family.

————

He doesn't remark unkindly on another's
accent, unfamiliarity with English, or
regional or cultural speech patterns.

————

He does not tell another child that
using "ain't" is bad grammar. It is
bad grammar, but it is not up to your
son to point that out.

————

He follows without hesitation the
practices and rules of conduct when
visiting someone else's home, such as
removing shoes before entering or not
feeding the dog from the table.

————

He bows his head and is respectful
of a blessing before a meal, wherever
and whenever it is said.

―――――

He does not make disparaging
remarks about the customs or
practices of another culture.

PARENT POINTERS

Use "Sir" and "Ma'am" in
appropriate situations if you require
its use from your son.

―――――

Do not require the use of "Sir" and
"Ma'am" from anyone other than your
own son if other children are not
in the habit of using it.

―――――

Do not discourage its use from boys
who do, even if your own son does not.
It is not appropriate to respond to a
young man's reply of "Yes, Ma'am" with a

shudder, an admonishment that you are not his grandmother, and an order not to do it again.

_____

Deliver a reminder, when needed, in a quiet and subtle manner. Veteran users of "Sir" and "Ma'am" report that once mastered, it becomes a life-long habit.

Try This At Home

If your son comes home from school and reports that an Indian child has joined his classroom, or he is invited to dine with a Korean family, do some research with him on the unfamiliar country and culture. There is a Muslim temple at the end of our street. About once a year they hold an open house, and before we attended for the first time, we went on the Internet to learn about their faith and protocol. It made the visit to an unfamiliar environment less intimidating and more interesting.

Some Good Advice

Before I moved to Nashville, I often traveled there on business. I was amazed by the extravagant displays of southern hospitality and countless invitations extended by people I barely knew to come by and see them the next time I was in town. When I moved here and bumped into these same people—people who had given me the impression that they were my future best friends—they were all pleasant and welcoming but none went so far as to extend a formal invitation for dinner. I finally asked a born-and-bred southern woman why southern hospitality had suddenly turned so inhospitable. She drawled with a laugh, "Why, Honey, we just love y'all until we find out you're stayin'!" She was being a tad facetious, but I learned not to interpret an unfamiliar culture using only my frame of reference.

Chapter Three

INTRODUCTIONS, GREETINGS, AND LEAVINGS

First impressions count, and the great majority of first impressions take place during introductions. More than once we have heard the advisory: You never get another chance to make a first impression. Young children are often given the benefit of the doubt, and even a terrible introductory meeting can be forgiven if the parent apologizes for his son's refusal to come out from behind his father's legs and take his thumb out of his mouth by explaining that Dylan missed his afternoon nap or hasn't had his dinner.

Even for grown-ups introductions can be tricky to navigate and easy to bumble. For children, particularly young or shy children, they can be extremely uncomfortable. In introducing your son to the practice of polite introductions, always keep his age and level of introversion or extroversion in mind.

Children do have another advantage over grown-ups when meeting someone for the first time: simply by not appearing sullen, young boys can be regarded as cute. A boy who does nothing more than smile and venture a shy "hello" might even be regarded as charming and well-mannered. A parent can expect little more than that from their three to five year old; once a boy enters the school system, where he will face more authority figures than before, he should know that a little more is expected of him. And by the time he is approaching double-digit years and his social circle has widened, he should have mastered the basics of responding to introductions.

Even the youngest of children can be exposed to the rituals and practices of proper introductions, but a fumbling introduction is better than none at all. It is extremely rude, when in a group of people, to encounter an acquaintance or colleague and not perform some type of introduction. If you have completely forgotten a name, you might forewarn the people you are with and hope that they can help you by introducing themselves first, prompting the one whose name you have forgotten to introduce himself as well. If that doesn't work, you may as well come clean and admit to your malfunctioning memory. If your son sees you practicing this basic form of social inclusion without exception, no matter how awkwardly executed it may be, he will come to see that it is normal and courteous behavior.

Very young boys can and should be introduced but not expected to do anything more than stand quietly while pleasantries are exchanged among the grown-ups. Keep in mind the minimal attention span of a very young boy, and do not expect that he maintain this demeanor while grown-ups discuss a protracted business deal or counsel each other on their midlife crises.

According to traditional etiquette there are three basic rules of introduction. The first two are fairly simple; the third can be more complicated, particularly in modern times when status is dictated by so many particulars. It would behoove parents to know these rituals and practices themselves:

1. A man is always introduced to a lady.

2. A young person is always introduced to an older person.

3. A less important person is always introduced to a more important person.

Fortunately, most of us will never be faced with the possibility of having to introduce Mick Jagger to Madonna—who would know? As a man, Mick Jagger should be introduced to Madonna, but as a younger person, Madonna should be introduced to Mick Jagger. And who's to say who is more important—Mick or Madonna? Surely they already know each other, so introductions are not necessary. In all other cases, it is best to remember these simple rules and adhere to them whenever possible.

When introducing a young child to an adult, age takes precedence over gender, so the child should always be introduced to the adult. "Sam, I'd like you to meet Reverend Hilley." "Mr. Hilley, this is my son Sam." A four-year-old boy will be confused and perhaps even frightened by an adult thrusting out a hand to be shaken, and considerate people do not put children in that position. A young boy can simply try his hardest to make eye contact and say hello.

Anticipating the handshaking formality, parents can rehearse with their son at home. Another rule of thumb is that an older person always extends his or her hand first to a younger one, so in the event that you have an extreme extrovert on your hands, do advise your outgoing son to wait and follow the adult's lead.

As a boy matures, it is most important to teach him the value of standing up straight, making eye contact, and speaking clearly. Slouching about and looking down at the floor or at an area somewhere over the introductee's shoulder implies that the young man is bored, has something to hide, or has something more important holding his interest. Eye contact is not a staring contest; it only takes two or three seconds, but the impression lasts much longer. (It should be noted that among Native Americans, it is considered rude to make direct eye contact with others.)

When a young man is introduced to a grown-up, he may respond with something simple: "Hello" is always preferred over "Hi," and is certainly better than "Hey" in the southern vernacular, or "Yo" in a northern one. If the person to whom your son is being introduced continues the conversation with "How are you?" he can say, "Fine," or even "Fine, thank you." A helpful lesson to be learned early on is that strangers do not really want to know if your head hurts or you have a toothache, but that "How are you?" is just another form of polite speech.

Boys older than seven or eight are capable of a brief conversation, maintaining eye contact, and speaking clearly and loudly enough for the elderly to hear him. A grown-up might say, "Where do you go to school?" and Aaron answers, "Alexander Hamilton Elementary." "And what grade are you in?" "I'm in the fifth grade." "Do you like school?" "Yes."

You may be tempted to answer for your child, particularly if he is slow or hesitant in responding. Resist this temptation, along with the urge to nudge, kick, or pinch him. Allow him to work through this—it's not nearly as bad as public speaking. Later, you might commend him for his mature interaction with your boss.

When the exchange is completed and you are leaving, a younger boy can simply say good-bye. A boy older than ten can be encouraged to add, "It was nice to meet you."

You Know You
Are Raising A Gentleman If . . .

He refers to an adult as Mr. Shaw
or Mrs. Shaw until he is asked
to do otherwise.

He is cordial and polite when
encountering your friends and
acquaintances in social situations.

When introduced to a stranger,
he stands and remains standing until
he is told to do otherwise.

He removes or at least tips the bill of his
ball cap when being introduced to an adult.

When he is the common denominator
between two or more strangers, he performs
introductions as efficiently as possible. He
uses the first and last names among peers. If
he is introducing a peer to a grown-up, he

refers to the grown-up as Mr., Mrs., or Ms.;
if he normally calls the grown-up only by
first name, he introduces him as Jeff Jones.

_____

When introducing members of his family
to others, he explains the relationship.
"This is my mother, Mrs. Campanis, and
my sister, Lindsay Campanis."

_____

He does not shudder in horror or turn his
cheek in disgust when an adult relative is
determined to hug or kiss him but simply
bears up as best he can. He will be
confronted with far more unappealing
social situations in his life.

PARENT POINTERS

Know the basic rules of introductions.

_____

Always make introductions when people
in a group do not know one another.

_____

Always include your son in the introductions, but do not require him to do more than he is comfortable doing.

———

Do not tell your son to kiss or hug someone when it has not been requested.

TRY THIS AT HOME

Make a game out of performing introductions, enlisting the aid of siblings, spouse, or friends. In one scenario you and your son are in a public place and you run across "the librarian" from your son's school. Allow your son to make the introductions: "Dad, this is Mrs. Stringfield, the librarian at my school. Mrs. Stringfield, this is my father, Ronnie Griffin."

Pretend you run into one of your employees at a baseball game. "David, this is John Thompson. He works in the graphics department at the office. John, this is my oldest son, David." David responds, "Hello, Mr. Thompson," and offers his hand if Mr.

Thompson offers his first. (Do not instruct a child to call you by your first name without consulting the child's parent first. Some parents prefer that their children address all adults with the proper titles.)

SOME GOOD ADVICE

When I was growing up, I spent at least one weekend a month at my maternal grandparents' house, which I always looked forward to. Even better, my mother's only sister, Donnie, still lived at home, and though she was seven years older than me, she always allowed me to tag along with her and her glamorous teenage girlfriends. The town they lived in was very small, and it seemed that Donnie knew everyone. In addition she was one of the friendliest people I have ever known, and without exception had at least a smile and a "hello" for everyone we came across. Her warm greeting to total strangers was sometimes met with surprise, but the eventual response was almost always a smile and a "hello" in return. I was a fairly shy child, but I absolutely adored my aunt and strove to do everything she did. She taught me early on that it's not so hard to smile and say hello, and that even the smallest gesture can inspire a big return.

Chapter Four

SHOPPING, OFFICES, AND WAITING ROOMS

When child care is unavailable, babies and pre-toddlers are fairly simple to tote about. Put them in a portable car seat, lay them in a carriage, strap them onto your chest, pack up the diaper bag, and off you go. Rarely will the appearance of your bundle of joy be greeted with anything less than delight, unless he is engaged in one of the following: loud and extended bouts of inexplicable and inconsolable crying, projectile vomiting, or an extremely odiferous diaper mess. A well-mannered parent remedies such situations at once, even if it means retreating to the car or returning home immediately.

Once your boy has taken his first steps, however, he will be much more difficult to confine. As soon as a boy is mobile, he must be taught the basics of good manners if he is to accompany his mother or father out in public. The first step in accomplishing this might be to convey the idea that going along to the dry cleaner, the grocery store, or the bank is not a burden, but an opportunity to spend time together. At least that's how I remember it.

I was the oldest of five children, all born within a space of nine years. My mother was a stay-at-home mom with an endless stream of tasks, and there was little one-on-one time with any of her children. Once a week she did her grocery shopping, and every one of us vied to be the chosen one who would tag along.

My father, in order to support a family of seven, worked one full-time and two part-time jobs, one of which was as a mechanic at a service station. From the time they were about seven years old, my father took my brothers with him to the service station on Saturday afternoons. There, they were expected to do little chores.

When not so engaged, they were allowed to sit with the men in the molded plastic chairs that sat in a line outside the entrance to the service station, get a bottle of pop, and listen to man talk. They spoke when spoken to but otherwise kept quiet and gave up their chair if another man needed it while waiting for his car. (Women did not darken the doors of service stations in those days . . . back when there were service stations.)

We felt special just for being allowed to share that time with our parents, and that privilege gave us a sense of responsibility for our behavior. Unlike teenagers, young children want to spend time with their parents, whether sitting down to hear a story, playing Chutes & Ladders, or going along to the bank. Errands might not be as much fun as playing a game, but children must eventually learn that even unpleasant things can be borne with as pleasant a nature as possible.

For quick errands such as banking, going to the post office, short shopping trips, or picking up material at an office, boys do not need to be provided with a diversion, but in all fairness, should be given as accurate an idea as possible of the duration of said errand. Children should never be required to accompany their mothers when buying shoes or their fathers when shopping for kitchen flooring. You are asking for trouble.

Children should not be expected to endure lengthy waits in a doctor's or dentist's waiting room without some type of diversion. Pediatrician offices usually come equipped with toys and books, but don't count on it. Pre-readers can carry a bag containing a coloring book, some small Matchbox cars, or a self-contained puzzle. Balls of any type are a bad idea anywhere but parks or gymnasiums. Older boys should be encouraged to bring a book, but Game Boys are another option, as long as that annoying sound is turned off.

If you must bring your child to the office with you while you meet with a colleague or complete a task, it is your responsibility to provide your child with something to occupy him, and it is your son's responsibility to remain focused on that task or pastime. Under no circumstances is he to touch things that do not belong to him or to rummage through someone's desk.

When shopping or doing other errands with his parent, a young man should be expected to stay within sight and not run willy-nilly up and down the cereal aisle while mother is in the dairy department. If the young man cannot control himself in the grocery store, he will have to ride in the cart until he can. This applies to ten year olds as well as four year olds.

At the check-out line, a young man does not badger his father for one of the sugary treats displayed at the child's eye view, though the manufacturers do their best to assure that children will. Make it clear immediately to the young man that badgering will not result in anything favorable, or you leave yourself open to a lifetime of badgering.

In stores, as in offices, children do not touch things that do not belong to them, which includes everything. Even if, or especially if, your child is in a stroller, this notion must be reinforced. I thought my three-year-old son and I were going to be hauled off to jail the afternoon we left an Eddie Bauer store and unbeknownst to me—until we were stopped by the mall security guard—my son had swiped a stainless steel coffee mug, a pricey pair of leather gloves, and a compass-tachometer, all of which were resting in his lap. Thankfully, we were simply asked to return the pilfered goods and make our apologies, and his budding criminal record was expunged.

You Know You Are Raising A Gentleman If . . .

He stays close by the adult on duty
in public places. This is good manners,
as it saves the adult from having to raise
his voice or chase the child about; it is
also a vital safety habit.

―――――

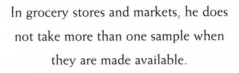

In grocery stores and markets, he does
not take more than one sample when
they are made available.

_____

He accidentally makes a mess in a
grocery store and informs a grown-up
so that the mess can be cleaned up.
He does not need to pick up the mess
himself or pay for any broken items.

_____

When forced to accompany his
mother or father on a clothing
buying expedition, he never peeks
under the dressing room wall to spy
on another customer.

_____

He does not mess up someone's desk,
rummage through one's drawers, use a
telephone, or log onto someone's computer
when at an office. He also asks permission
before eating or drinking anything.

_____

He occupies just one seat in the waiting room close by his parent. If the waiting room is crowded and another adult needs a seat, the young gentleman gets up and takes a small, unobtrusive spot on the floor.

———

In waiting rooms, he does not hog all the books or puzzles but takes just one as he needs it, then returns it to the pile when he is finished.

———

He uses trash receptacles in public places. A young gentleman does not leave a candy wrapper or used tissue on a chair in a waiting room or a counter in a bank.

Parent Pointers

Do not expect a child to endure a lengthy shopping trip unless it is to a toy or candy store.

———

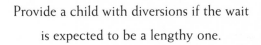

Provide a child with diversions if the wait
is expected to be a lengthy one.

———

Give the child an accurate idea of
how long the errands will take.
Telling a child that the rounds of
post office, dry cleaner, bank,
and appliance repair store will
"just be a few minutes" is
misleading at best.

———

Do not promise a reward at the outset, but
if a successful trip is accomplished, offer
some small token of appreciation for his
good behavior and manners.

TRY THIS AT HOME

In spite of your best instructions, and your son's
best intentions, there is a good chance that sooner
or later you and your son may get separated in a
mall, department store, movie theater, or market.
Practice at home what your child should do if he

gets separated from his parent: find an employee or security guard, tell that person he is lost, and stay put until his parent is found.

Some Good Advice

No matter how tempting it is not to drag a small child into the post office to buy a book of stamps or the grocery store to get a carton of milk, never leave children under the age of ten in a parked car alone. The unlikely, but still possible, consequences are not worth the inconvenience. Never leave any child in a running car; a lunge to turn up the radio can disengage a car from the parked position with tragic results.

Chapter Five

PLAYGROUNDS, PLAYDATES, AND PLAYING WELL WITH OTHERS

When my mother was raising her children, there was no such thing as playdates. Mothers got together in someone's kitchen for coffee at least one morning a week. Naturally, they brought their babies and toddlers along. Babies were held in laps or deposited in playpens while the mothers chit-chatted, drank coffee, and ate cake. Toddlers were deposited in a nearby room of the house—probably not even child-proofed—or the backyard, where they remained until someone was bitten or pushed down, the coffee ran out, or it was naptime.

Older children—school age for example— were shooed out of their house to run or bike to their friends' houses, where those mothers shooed them back outside as well. There they remained until they were called home for meals or bed. Life was simpler then.

Today, with so many mothers working outside of the home, coffee klatches aren't as common. Neighborhoods aren't what they used to be, and the world isn't as safe as it once was, or at least seemed at the time. Hence, we have "playdates."

When a young man goes to another child's home for a playdate, he does not tote along a toy chest full of his own things, as if expecting that his date will not have the caliber of amusements and diversions to which he is accustomed. The exception would be that if plans have been made to ride tricycles or bicycles or to rollerblade; then the visiting boy brings his own equipment. A host does not ride his bike if he cannot provide one for his friend or if his friend did not bring his own.

A young man treats another child's toys as if they were his own, assuming that he is not destructive with his own toys. If a toy is accidentally broken, a young man apologizes and allows the parents to devise a solution, if one is necessary. A good guest follows the rules of the host home when he is visiting. When the playdate is over, visitors help the host clean up.

If a young man is hosting another child in his home, he is prepared to share his toys. If he owns something that would devastate him to lose, put that toy or possession away before the guest arrives. If a toy is accidentally broken, a young man accepts his guest's apology graciously. The host defers to the guest's wishes with regard to play; when a compromise cannot be reached, sometimes it is necessary for a parent to intervene.

A good host occasionally inquires if his guest is thirsty or would like a snack. The host does not correct another child on his manners but may point out that his mother does not allow children's drinks in the living room. Further, a host quickly and emphatically tells his guest that they do not swing their kitty by the tail or let the snake out of its cage. When he has company, the host does not engage in exclusionary play such as Game Boy or computer solitaire. A young gentleman helps his friends clean up, but if his guest does not, a gentleman host does not insist.

Many mothers of young children form mothers' groups or playgroups. From the time my children were babies until they began school, I was in a group of about eight mothers and, eventually, sixteen children. From early spring to late fall, we met every Thursday morning at a child-friendly park equipped with paved trails, a small playground, a large sandy area, plenty of grass, and picnic tables. Everyone packed a lunch and blankets, and for the next three hours—or until complete child meltdown—the mothers engaged in adult conversation covering subjects that ranged from potty training to politics. Field trials proved to us that young boys are more aggressive than young girls, and some lessons must be more assertively enforced. Under our collective eye,

our children were taught the rules of fair play
on a playground. The most common rules are:

Young gentlemen do not push other children
down.

They do not throw toys, sticks, rocks, or sand
at another child.

They do not snatch toys from other children.

They do not spit water on other children
when drinking from the water fountain.

They wait their turn in line for the slide or
climbing stations.

They do not push other children in an attempt
to speed them up.

They do not hog the swings but take turns. If
a boy is too young to assess an appropriate
length of time for a turn, an adult should set
and enforce limits.

They do not take another child's riding vehicles without permission.

They do not knock down another child's sand castle or mud fort.

They do not form small cliques with the purpose of excluding other children. The exception is Boys Only clubs. Girls are then free to organize Girls Only clubs.

YOU KNOW YOU ARE RAISING A GENTLEMAN IF . . .

He does not invite a friend over
for a playdate without first checking
with his parents.

———

He does not invite himself for a playdate.

———

He does not say dismissive things
about another child's toys, home,
or electronic equipment.

———

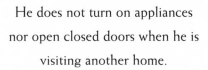

He does not turn on appliances
nor open closed doors when he is
visiting another home.

_____

He does not announce that he is hungry
or ask for something to eat; he may,
however, ask politely for a glass
of water if he is thirsty.

_____

He does not search willy-nilly through the
house for a bathroom but asks where it is.

_____

He uses the bathroom with the door
closed, and he flushes and washes his
hands when finished.

_____

He tells the parent on duty when
he doesn't feel well.

_____

He does not leave the host home or yard
without telling a grown-up.

_____

He helps smaller children on the playground.

_____

He helps carry his things to
the car when the time comes to leave
the playground or park. When it is time to
leave, a young gentleman comes when
called and does not run off into the
woods or wrap his legs around the
fireman's pole and refuse to go.

PARENT POINTERS

Always make arrangements for a playdate with
the other parents, not through the children.

_____

Set a definite time for the playdate, provide
a number where you can be reached, and
pick your child up when you say you will.

_____

If you have not met the parents of your
son's playdate, introduce yourself; do not
let your child out in front of the house.

_____

Provide a change of clothing if bathroom accidents are still a possibility.

_____

Always inform the other parent of a child's allergies or idiosyncrasies (e.g., "Neil cannot eat peanuts and is subject to nosebleeds, and here is how it should be handled").

_____

Never send a sick child to another child's home.

_____

Do not allow a sick child to participate in a playgroup.

_____

Make clear your family rules on appropriate play toys, movies, computer play, television, video games, and snacks.

_____

Gently enforce your house rules in your car or home (e.g., "We do not use the words 'shut up' and 'stupid' or curse in our house").

_____

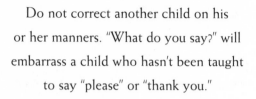

Do not correct another child on his
or her manners. "What do you say?" will
embarrass a child who hasn't been taught
to say "please" or "thank you."

———

Do not punish another child for
unacceptable behavior, but you can
stop it (e.g., "I cannot allow you to hit
Dylan with the stick"). Depending on the
extreme nature of the behavior, mention it
without recrimination to the child's parent.

———

Remove your son from the
playgroup for inappropriate or
unacceptable behavior. Imploring him
not to bite rather than placing him in
time-out is not doing anyone a favor. If
the unacceptable behavior continues,
skip one of the playgroup sessions
until your child can control himself.

———

Reciprocate an invitation to play at another child's house with one to play at yours.

TRY THIS AT HOME

Before a playgroup date have a private talk with your child about including everyone in the fun. Ask him to think about how he would feel if he were left out and how sad you would feel for him. Ask him if he would want to be party to hurting another child's feelings. Anticipate what he might do if others in the group want to leave out another child. Help him figure out ways to include everyone.

SOME GOOD ADVICE

Because his mother and I were friends, I wanted my son to be friends with her son. What I didn't acknowledge was that my son and her son, even at a very young age, had very little in common. My son is very athletic; hers is not. Her son collected Pokémon cards; mine couldn't care less. Her son was learning chess; mine had no interest. Every time we visited each other, Harry's behavior became increasingly rude. One afternoon when my son deliberately kicked a ball that hit my friend's son squarely in his back, I hauled him inside and asked him what he was thinking. He fairly hissed at me, "I am thinking I don't like J. J.!" He expressed himself inappropriately, but he had certainly been sending signals for some time that I had ignored. No matter how much you want it to happen, children should never be forced into friendships with children they don't like or with whom they have nothing in common. However, they should learn to be polite and cordial when around people with whom they share few interests.

Chapter Six

SLEEPOVERS: FRIENDS AND RELATIVES

One of the great measures of independence in your son's life will be his first sleepover. When is he ready? It's easier to say when he is not.

He is not ready to sleep over at a friend's house if he has not mastered the basics of feeding himself, brushing his teeth, washing himself, and dressing himself. Nor is he ready if he isn't sleeping through the night or if he is still having occasional bedwetting incidents. In general, boys suffer bedwetting accidents at more advanced ages than girls, so you must be extremely cognizant of this as it is not so much a matter of manners as one of self-esteem. If you have the slightest doubt, it is not worth the humiliation your child will suffer waking up in a friend's home on a wet sheet. If your son thinks he is ready, talk to him beforehand about what to do if an accident happens: he should inform the host parent rather than hurriedly make the bed, hide his nightclothes, and hope no one notices. It is up to his friend and the friend's parents to treat him with the compassion he deserves. If it should happen in your home with a visiting child, do not make a big deal of the incident. Assure him that accidents happen to everyone and get him into a clean set of clothes. You should wash his nightclothes along with the sheets and divert the children's attention as quickly and cheerfully as possible to something else: a special breakfast, Saturday morning cartoons, or outside play. Have a private, thoughtful, and emphatic talk with your own child at the earliest opportunity to be sure he understands that it was an accident, that his friend probably feels ashamed, and that it is something that is to remain completely private and not to be spoken of again. Invite that child over again soon to let him know that he is still welcome in your home.

When your son is ready for a sleepover at a friend's house, he packs a backpack with the basics: nightclothes, clean underwear, two changes of clean clothes, toothbrush, toothpaste, hairbrush, any medications he is required to take, a sleep toy if he uses one (e.g., stuffed animal or blanket), and in some cases, a pillow and sleeping bag. He may also bring a book and one or two small toys, but not his entire plastic animal kingdom.

A young gentleman follows his host's bedtime rules and does not whine that he is always allowed to stay up until midnight on weekends when he is at home. The host parent leaves some type of nightlight on that can guide the child to a bathroom should he wake up in the middle of the night. A child's parents warn the host parents if their child is in the habit of falling out of bed or sleepwalking.

A young gentleman also follows the host house rules when he gets up in the morning. My son will sleep as late as 8 A.M. on Saturday mornings, but his friend Aaron wakes up at dawn. One of the most considerate things I have ever seen was Aaron sitting quietly in bed at 6:30 on a Saturday morning with a flashlight on his book as my own son snored beside him. I wanted to give him a medal.

If a guest in your home wants to go home, do not make him feel ashamed of being homesick. Likewise, if your child is tentative about spending the night away, assure him that he may call you if necessary.

The first time each of my children had sleepovers planned with friends, I got emotional as I packed their little bags, drove them over to their friend's house, and waved bye-bye to their rapidly retreating backs as they raced off to play, completely thrilled at the idea of spending a night away from Mom. I didn't hear a peep again until the next day when their friend's parent brought them home all smiles and full of stories about their great adventure. And that's a good thing; logically I knew that their independence was a healthy sign of their self-confidence and security. In my sentimental mother's eye, however, I was already seeing them loading up their Toyotas and heading off to college without a backward glance. Hopefully, when that day arrives, they will do it with the same sense of adventure and confidence that they took with them on their first sleepover.

You Know You Are Raising A Gentleman If . . .

He keeps his belongings in the proper places and cleans up his space.

———

He leaves the bathroom as he found it—seat down, water off, towels hung up.

———

He does not touch or use things that do not belong to him.

———

He conforms to house rules and schedules.

―――

He informs his hosts immediately if he
has an accident of any kind.

―――

He shows a guest around the house, and
lets him know where the bathroom,
telephone, and exits are located.

―――

He asks his guest what he
would like to do.

―――

He does not make fun of his guest
if he has an accident, sleeps with a
blankie, still sucks his thumb, or suffers
a sudden bout of homesickness and
needs to call his mother.

―――

He thanks his host for having him
or his guest for coming.

―――

Parent Pointers

Make sure your guests know where the
bathroom and emergency exits are.

_____

Have phone numbers of the
guest's parents and their whereabouts
for the evening.

_____

Share your child's physician's name
and insurance carrier, as well as hospital
preference, in the unlikely event
of an extreme emergency and you
cannot be reached.

_____

Share your child's allergies or medical
conditions (e.g., the proper use of an
inhaler if your child has asthma).

_____

Inform the host of any sleeping problems
your child might have, such as:
sleepwalking, restlessness, early riser.

_____

Let the host know that if your child suffers
an inconsolable bout of homesickness, you
are available by phone or to pick him
up, no matter the hour.

———

A divorced parent does not have the
person he or she is dating spend the night
when the children are at home. Period.
Call me Dr. Laura; I don't care.

TRY THIS AT HOME

The first time my son had a friend spend the
night, the friend decided right around bedtime
that he needed to go home. He didn't seem too
upset, just a little apprehensive about going to
sleep in a strange bed. I told him that would be
fine if that was what he wanted and asked him
if he would like me to call his parents. I spoke
to them first and assured them he wasn't
hysterical but just seemed unsure. I asked them
what his normal bedtime routine was, and they
told me that one of them usually got into bed

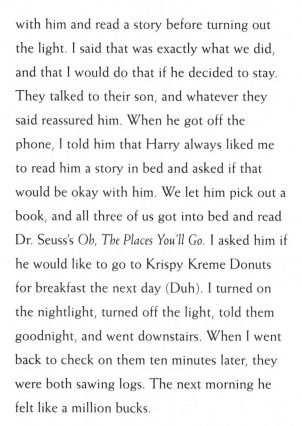

with him and read a story before turning out the light. I said that was exactly what we did, and that I would do that if he decided to stay. They talked to their son, and whatever they said reassured him. When he got off the phone, I told him that Harry always liked me to read him a story in bed and asked if that would be okay with him. We let him pick out a book, and all three of us got into bed and read Dr. Seuss's *Oh, The Places You'll Go*. I asked him if he would like to go to Krispy Kreme Donuts for breakfast the next day (Duh). I turned on the nightlight, turned off the light, told them goodnight, and went downstairs. When I went back to check on them ten minutes later, they were both sawing logs. The next morning he felt like a million bucks.

SOME GOOD ADVICE

There are all kinds of first sleepovers. While most of us think of them as exciting occasions when our children visit friends or relatives, when parents are divorcing sleepovers can be traumatic. Until my ex-husband, our children, and I attended a course called "Children Facing Divorce," I didn't know the exact nature of the fears my children experienced the first few months they spent the night at their father's new home. As it turned out, they were deeply concerned about what I would do while they were gone, how lonely I might be, and if I were safe at home alone.

If you are facing this situation, discuss this in advance with your children. Tell them that you will miss them, but that you have plans and that you know they will have a great time with their other parent. It would be wise for you to have a friend over the first time your child spends the night with the other parent. Take my word for it, it will be miserable and you will need all the support you can get.

Chapter Seven

PARTY MANNERS

If you thought your social calendar was full before, you will be absolutely agog at what happens once you have children. In addition to your own engagements, your mailbox will soon be brimming with invitations addressed to your child, who hardly seems old enough to be getting his own mail. Most will be of the birthday party ilk, but you will also soon be subject to a stream of summons to an array of family-friendly gatherings and countless opportunities to celebrate children.

One family I know invited sixteen children— and their respective thirty-two parents—to their little boy's first birthday party. It was not a pretty sight.

Dressed in their finest party clothes, the children were cute, for all of five minutes. Then one started crying, setting off a horrific chain reaction. Many were teething and drooling like St. Bernards. Most were in the first stages of walking, tottering precariously about the room until falling over and bopping their heads.

The parents had engaged a clown who succeeded in terrifying all sixteen children, particularly the birthday boy. The present-opening ceremony went on and on, with not a single child, including Prince Charming, paying one whit of attention. Finally, it was time for the birthday cake. As his parents urged him to blow out the candles and a dozen cameras flashed simultaneously in the poor child's eyes, he chose that very moment to loudly and unmistakably defecate. Whose crazy idea was this anyway?

I am of the opinion that with the exception of immediate family gatherings, children should not have birthday parties until they are at least three years old, and it is unrealistic to expect good party manners from your child until he is about five years old, which is about the youngest age parents can drop their son off at a birthday party and not be expected to stay. (Do not drop a child off without going into the party location and checking in with the parents.)

When your child receives an invitation to a birthday party, it is your responsibility to RSVP promptly. A young gentleman arrives promptly at the party or pre-arranges a late arrival if a soccer or baseball game conflicts. Once a child accepts an invitation to one party, he cannot reject that offer for another.

On arrival a young gentleman finds the guest of honor and wishes him a happy birthday. Unless he has some physical restrictions that prevent him from doing so, he participates in all party activities; the party is for the birthday child, and by accepting the invitation to the party he has made a tacit agreement to be a cheerful guest.

A young gentleman does not thrust his present in the birthday boy's face, nor does he make disparaging comments about the other gifts. When the cake is presented, he does not shove other boys out of his way to sit beside the birthday boy but takes the first available seat at the table. A guest does not assist in blowing out the candles unless it is requested, and he does not ask for the biggest slice of cake or the piece with the special décor.

When the party is over, he again wishes the guest of honor a happy birthday and thanks him and the parents for being invited.

A birthday boy should assist with the planning of his own party as long as he has realistic expectations. Many parents use the formula of one guest per each year of the child's age; a five year old can invite five friends, a ten year old can ask ten.

When his guests arrive, the birthday boy greets everyone and makes them all feel welcome. When opening his presents, the guest of honor acknowledges the giver, shows the opened gift to the audience, and offers sincere thanks. He never says, "I don't play with Legos

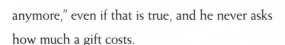

anymore," even if that is true, and he never asks how much a gift costs.

Besides birthday parties, there will be other opportunities for boys to attend family-inclusive parties from Christmas to the Fourth of July to joyous celebrations such as weddings.

If children are invited to the wedding and reception, it will be noted on the invitation. In most cases boys can wear what they would wear to church or temple. If there is a receiving line, boys can accompany their parents and just say hello. Children younger than six should not be permitted to carry plates through the buffet line but can point out what they would like. Boys six and older can carry their own plate but should not treat a privately-funded buffet like an all-you-can-eat breakfast bar.

There is no reason for a young man to wait for everyone to be seated until he eats; he should not take his used plate back to the buffet for a second helping.

When toasts are offered, he may either remain

in his seat or stand with the rest of the guests. If there is dancing, a young man should dance with his mother or grandmother, if they so desire. A young gentleman is under no obligation to ask girls his age to dance, but if he chooses to sit out that portion of the celebration, he does not snicker and make fun of those who participate.

In private homes where seating is at a minimum, a young gentleman does not take a chair when it would prevent an adult from sitting. Instead, he finds a spot on the floor as long as it is not within a walking path or a step on a staircase.

A friend of mine passed along her annual Easter egg hunt to us eight years ago when her own children got a little long in the tooth for the Easter Bunny. It is a very casual affair with about seventy-five children and fifty adults. The children play in the yard, then hunt for the eggs, then everyone spreads blankets on the lawn and collects a plate of food from the buffet.

While the guest list has remained consistent

from year to year, my children, as they have gotten older, have typically invited several new friends. They know it is their responsibility to make sure everyone is included in the fun, and that they will get the evil eye from their mother if even one child is spotted alone or not picked for a spot on one of the kickball teams. It must be working; after the party this year, a first-year Easter egg hunt mother sought me out to tell me how lovely my son had been to her three children, introducing them to the other kids, making sure they were included in the game, giving them egg-hunting tips, and making a place for them on his blanket. I made a mental note to go back to the store and get the jumbo chocolate bunny.

You Know You Are Raising A Gentleman If . . .

He does not talk about a party he is having, or was invited to, in front of other children who are not invited.

——

He does not go on and on about a party
he has attended or given in front of
people who were not there.

———

He greets and bids farewell to the
guest of honor, and thanks his host for
including him. He does the same to
the guest of honor's parents.

———

He greets, bids farewell to,
and thanks his guests for coming.

———

He never tries to steal the spotlight at
another boy's birthday party.

———

He does not ask for more of
anything—drinks, pizza, cake, or arcade
tokens—unless it is offered.

———

He never says, "I already have this,"
when opening a present.

———

He does not screw up his face
and say, "Gross, no way!" if his mother,
or grandmother, should ask him to
briefly sway across the dance floor
with her at a wedding.
Mothers and grandmothers get
sentimental at these affairs.

―――

When and if a young lady is so bold as
to ask him to dance, and he would rather
undergo a root canal than embarrass
himself in front of a hundred people,
he still accepts and endures.

Parent Pointers

Send party invitations in the mail.

―――

Instruct your son not to talk about his
own party, or a friend's party, in front
of other children.

―――

If a soccer game or swim meet will delay your son's arrival at a birthday party by more than thirty minutes, be sure that a late arrival is all right with the hosts. If the delay would be longer than sixty minutes, decline the invitation.

———

Keep track of who gave which gift so that mention may be made in the thank-you notes.

———

Be on time to pick children up after the party is over. Inform the hosting parents that you are taking your child.

———

Do not send extra money with your son to a birthday party held in any place with video games, air hockey, or foozball; it would not do for your son to be playing skeeball while everyone else is going into the movie theater.

———

Be clear about rules of the buffet table;
whatever he puts on his plate, he is
expected to eat. That means *one* dessert.

———

In hosting, let your son participate as
much as possible in the planning,
execution, and clean-up of the party.

———

Suggest ways that your son can be sure
everyone is included, particularly children
who don't know other children.

Try This At Home

Here's a possible birthday party scenario with
the potential for hurt feelings that you can discuss
beforehand: your son opens a gift, and it is
something he already has. He does not mention
this but just says thank you. If it cannot be returned
after the party, he can give it to a sibling or a
charity. If at the same party he opens a duplicate
gift, he just says thank you and moves on.

Some Good Advice

At the beginning of the school year, my son's kindergarten teacher sent home a list of dos and don'ts for parents. The most thoughtful one was not to send birthday party invitations to school with your child in the interest of saving postage or time unless the entire class is invited. As you will find out, notes sent home with a child, unless in an official school folder, will often remain crumpled up at the bottom of their backpack for months. More importantly, the children not invited might suffer serious feelings of rejection, and it can put your own child in an awkward situation if a left-out child asks why he was not invited.

Chapter Eight

DINING IN AND OUT

Every family photo album contains at least one series of pictures chronicling a child's early attempts at self-feeding. Typically, the child— his face, his hair, his ears, his hands, his clothes, the high chair, and anything else within a five-foot radius of him—will be covered with whatever he is attempting to get from the high chair tray to his mouth: spaghetti, macaroni and cheese, oatmeal, pudding, birthday cake. Just precious.

Then the process of training a child to get the food into his mouth begins in earnest. With much patience and practice your child will develop a working relationship with his fork.

Every young gentleman, as soon as he is able to reach a sink, even if it requires the aid of a stepping stool, washes his hands before coming to the table. Once he is at the table, seated on a chair or booster seat, the simplest things go a long way towards fostering pleasant dining experiences. Even a young gentleman can be taught not to play with his food, not to chew with his mouth open, not to talk with his mouth full, and to keep his elbows off the table. If parents insist on these common courtesies with consistent reinforcement, they need not fear boorish behavior from their son when the family has company over, dines out, or when their son has dinner at a friend's house.

The adoption of more complicated tools and sophisticated skills comes next. The napkin is not intended for use as a paper airplane, a hat, a mask, or a place to deposit chewing gum (always dispose of chewing gum before coming to the table). A young gentleman places his napkin on his lap after being seated and uses it to wipe his mouth and fingers during and after the meal.

No matter how utterly famished he is, a young gentleman waits until everyone is seated before digging into his food. In homes where grace is said, eating begins after giving thanks for the food.

If a young gentleman desires something that is out of his reach, he does not do the boardinghouse reach. Instead he asks: "May I have the butter, please?" or "Please pass the gravy".

A young gentleman is given a knife only when he has reasonably mastered its use. Once he is able to cut his own meat or butter his own biscuits, he places the dirty knife on his plate when not in use, not on the table.

A young gentleman must always remember that unless the meal is brought to his front door by a person wearing a uniform, is delivered via a drive-through window, or comes out of plastic or Styrofoam containers, someone in the house has gone to some degree of effort to create a nutritious and delicious meal. A young gentleman does not sit down at the table, look at his plate, and say, "Eeeeew, what's this?"

All parents—even the most sophisticated gourmands—will discover that young taste buds are narrowly defined, and for some time will only respond favorably to foods that can be covered with ketchup, syrup, or melted cheese. Over time this will change as they continue to be exposed to new foods. My son hated spinach, broccoli, and peas until he turned six or seven; now he can't get enough. I do not subscribe to the notion of making children eat things they don't like. Children have very distinct likes and dislikes predicated on everything from color to texture. As a child, I hated peas because of the unpleasant sensation of the squish of the inner pea into my mouth.

A young gentleman does not gobble his food as if it were his last meal but maintains a good pace by observing his fellow diners. When a young gentleman is finished eating, he asks to be excused before leaving the table.

Dining out with children in full-service restaurants is always an adventure and one for which parents should be sure they are ready. While many diners greet the arrival of children in a restaurant as they would a swarm of mosquitoes, the fact of the matter is that children have every right to dine at family-friendly restaurants. Their fellow diners have every right to expect those children to behave and not to interfere with their neighbors' dining enjoyment. Restaurants that employ *maître d's*, *sommeliers*, and Reidel stemware are probably not suitable for children.

When dining out, the same basic rules of the home apply, but even more so. Because there are other people about, a young gentleman does not raise his voice at the table. He has good posture and does not loll about at the buffet table. Unlike at home, where he is called to dinner when it is ready, in a restaurant there is always a wait for food. Many family restaurants provide crayons, place mats, and small games to help children pass the interminable fifteen minutes of downtime, but parents should also be prepared with even something as simple as a small pad of paper.

By the time a young man attends his first formal dinner in an upscale restaurant, at a party, or in a home, he should know the basic rules of bread plates, silverware, and passing:

Your bread plate is the smaller one to the left above the forks. (The salad plate is larger, and also to the left of the place setting or on top of the dinner plate.)

A young gentleman takes one piece of bread from a basket without fingering the others then passes the basket along to the right. Likewise, he takes one pat of butter from the butter dish (with a butter knife if one is provided) then passes the butter plate to the right.

The silverware furthest away from the plate is used first. When a course is completed, a young man puts his used silverware on the plate.

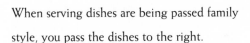

When serving dishes are being passed family style, you pass the dishes to the right.

You Know You Are Raising A Gentleman If . . .

He washes his hands before
coming to the table.

―――

He comes to the table properly attired.

―――

He keeps all four legs of his
chair on the floor.

―――

He does not reach across
his dining companions for the salt
and pepper shakers.

―――

He does not take the
last helping without offering it
to someone else.

―――

He does not eat before the
others begin, before his host is seated,
or before the blessing.

———

He asks to be excused from
the table to go to the rest room or
when he has finished eating.

———

He does not ask
what's for dessert while everyone
is still eating the salad.

———

When dining out in a restaurant, he does
not get up from the table and wander
about, nor does he create bizarre and
potentially explosive concoctions from
the condiments on the table.

———

He treats the server cordially and
with respect, saying "Thank you,"
when his meal is delivered.

Parent Pointers

Teach by example and always,
even during the most casual meals,
follow basic dining etiquette.

———

Do not ask children or guests to say the
blessing unless you know they are
comfortable with it.

———

Do not force children to eat what
they don't like but encourage
them to take a taste.

———

Never argue at the dinner table;
if you are having a squabble, put it
on hold during the meal.

———

Do not watch television during dinner.

———

Do not engage in lengthy phone
conversations during dinner.

———

Do not talk on your cell phone at a table in a restaurant. If an emergency occurs, get up from the table and go outside to take the call.

———

Treat servers and professional help with respect. If the meal or service is not satisfactory, ask to see a manager and make your complaints discreetly.

———

Always compliment and thank the host or hostess when invited to dine in another's home.

TRY THIS AT HOME

If a parent spends time and effort cooking a meal, the worst thing a young gentleman can do is greet the serving of the meal with one of the following: "Eeeew," "Gross," "Yuck," or "What's *that?*" A young man should not be surprised if his mother picks up his plate, throws its contents down the sink, and shrieks at him to go to his room for the rest of the night. While this is an understandable reaction, it does little to promote empathy in or improved behavior from a little boy.

Try this instead. Pick up the crooked little coffee mug your son made for you with his own two little hands last Mother's Day. No doubt he will remember the tears that sprang to your eyes and the huge fuss that rewarded its presentation. Ask him how he would have felt had you opened his gift and said, "Eeeeew, what's *this?*" Explain to him that the beauty of the coffee mug is immensely enhanced by the fact that he made it just for you, because you are his mother, and he loves you. Tell him you do not expect applause when you set a meal on the table, but that it hurts your feelings when he recoils as if you had set a plate of cow manure before him. I bet he gets the message.

SOME GOOD ADVICE

Do not force a child to eat something he hates. My mother, a child of the Depression, believed you should eat whatever was set before you—all of it. This was terribly painful for my little sister, who hated everything that had ever had any contact with soil. Long after everyone else had left the table, poor Carolyn would be sitting there, forcing down the last of her peas and carrots, green beans, and boiled cabbage. One night just as she finished choking down the last mouthful of pureed butternut squash, her dire warnings to my mother were fulfilled; every bit of squash and everything else she had eaten that day came back up all over her plate, the table, the floor, and Carolyn. It was disgusting, but ultimately, thanks to her colorful exhibition, she saved all of us from the terrible plate-cleaning ordeal.

Chapter Nine

CULTURAL AFFAIRS: THE THEATER, MOVIES, SPORTS, MUSEUMS, AND LIBRARIES

When your children are very small, cultural events will likely be limited to movie theaters showing sixty-minute animated films, story hours in the children's section of bookstores and public libraries, and the occasional puppet show. Once they are mobile and talking, parents must enforce self-control from their youngsters during the performance, no matter how many unruly heathens are running about unfettered. It is not up to you to police other children, though you can certainly try to lead by example. Young boys must remain in their seats and not disturb the viewing enjoyment of others by standing up or disturb their listening enjoyment with loud talking.

As they get older, they will have occasion to

frequent performances, events, and cultural institutions that require more refined manners and a more mature level of behavior. The first step in promoting good audience manners is making certain a boy is old enough to enjoy the experience or at least endure it with a minimum of fidgeting. You will not foster a love of the ballet by dragging along a reluctant young man who would rather spend an hour at the orthodontist than sit through *The Nutcracker*. In fact, it may do more harm than good. Good behavior comes naturally when a child is enchanted by what is taking place before him. A young gentleman may never develop a love for the opera, but he is expected to exhibit a healthy respect for the efforts and skills of the artists and craftsmen behind the production. Anyone can bear anything for three hours, and it is good training for the future when he will have to endure far worse.

Children's theater is a wonderful introduction to the stage. The productions are lively, often including audience participation, and most importantly, they are short. Al fresco theatre such as Shakespeare in the Park is another fine way to ease children into the pleasures of the play. If the dialogue onstage sails over their heads, a bored young gentleman can occupy himself by lying on his back and gazing at the stars.

Once it has been determined that a child is old enough to sit relatively still for two to three hours and plans are made to attend a play, the opera, a symphony concert, or the ballet, a young gentleman should be told what to expect and what is expected of him.

For a live production of any type, members of the audience arrive on time in order to be seated before the performance begins; it is exceedingly rude to come in after the curtain has risen. If they are tardy, they must wait quietly in the back of the theatre until an usher finds the opportunity to seat them. A young gentleman visits the water fountain and rest room before being seated. If his seat is in the center of the row and others are already seated, he says "excuse me" as he approaches and allows them to stand to let him pass or shift their knees out of his way, in which case he must be very conscious of toes. He passes facing them, squeezing his bottom against the seats in the other row. If he is already seated and someone needs to move past him, he should tuck his feet under his chair and make sure the floor is clear in front of him.

He does not eat popcorn or candy or slurp soda during the performance as he might at a movie or a sporting event. During intermission, he may go to the lobby with his parents or guardian, and enjoy a refreshment if it is offered to him.

A young gentleman does not talk during the performance. If he must ask a question, he whispers into the ear of his mother or father. He does not emit extravagant and dramatic sighs of ennui, and he covers his mouth when he yawns. He does not flip loudly through the program or use it as a fan; wiggle in his seat or swing his legs and kick the seat in front of him; stand up and move about. He follows the lead

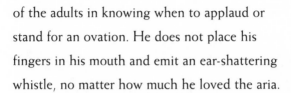

of the adults in knowing when to applaud or stand for an ovation. He does not place his fingers in his mouth and emit an ear-shattering whistle, no matter how much he loved the aria.

Attending a movie is a far more casual outing than a ballet or opera, but the most basic rules of courtesy, involving unnecessary talking and standing still apply. If he has seen the movie before but his companions have not, he does not tell them the end or announce just before a crucial scene: "Ooooo, watch him fall off the side of the cliff!" A young gentleman does not throw Raisinettes at his classmate sitting two rows in front of him, stick his hand in someone else's popcorn bucket without invitation, suck on a straw or crunch ice loudly, or rest his food and drink in the row where he might inadvertently kick it over and send a river of Dr. Pepper down to the front of the theater. If a young gentleman has set his food on the floor in front of him, and someone passing down the aisle knocks it over, he does not berate that

person. When the movie is over, a young gentleman picks up his trash and deposits it in the
garbage can located by the door of the theatre.

Attending a sporting event is a great
opportunity to admire the remarkable skills
of highly trained and disciplined athletes,
professional or otherwise. For many men, it
also seems to be a natural opportunity to release
one's frustrations and backed-up testosterone.
Witness the popularity of professional
wrestling. The judgment of parents who take
young boys to such spectacles of boorish,
violent, and sexist behavior is curious indeed,
and one assumes they are not there to learn
gentlemanly behavior. Most other sports, while
not as stringent in their rules of conduct as the
ballet, do require some decorum and courtesy.

A young gentleman gets to his seat without
disturbing fellow spectators, being careful not
to hit anyone in the eye with a foam-rubber
tomahawk or knock over a six-dollar beer. He
keeps his belongings in his lap or under his seat,

including binoculars, baseball gloves, pennants, and banners with which he hopes to attract the eye of the television cameras. He stands for the singing of the national anthem, always removing his hat. Once the game begins, he sits and remains seated unless a spectacular play occurs, and everyone stands for a better look, or during baseball's seventh inning stretch. In other sports it is fine to stand, stretch, and move about between quarters or periods. With respect to fellow spectators, a young gentleman does not get up to go to the rest room or concession stand or try to return to his seat during play but waits for a natural break in the action. A young gentleman does not scatter the remnants of his food and beverage about him—no one wants to step into a pile of leftover nachos—but scoots them under the seat until he can deposit them in a garbage can.

In spite of the behavior of many grown men, buying a ticket to a sporting event does not entitle a young man to scream insults at the players or the opposite team. Likewise, the practice of cheering on hockey players as they pummel one another is disturbing.

When visiting a library, a young gentleman follows the traditional rules of quiet respect for others and a certain reverence for the institution itself. In museums other than those geared specifically to small children, he moves quietly and calmly from room to room in the normal flow of traffic. He stands far enough back from the exhibit to allow others to see. He does not read the descriptions of the pieces aloud unless he is assisting a non-reader, in which case he should do it as quietly as possible. He never touches museum pieces. He does not lie down upon the benches for a quick snooze, no matter how bored he may be.

YOU KNOW YOU ARE RAISING A GENTLEMAN IF . . .

He removes his hat during a performance
in a theatre without being told to do so.

———

He disposes of his chewing gum
before a live performance.

———

He removes his ball cap during the
playing of the national anthem.

———

He doesn't cheer when a member
of an opposing team is hurt, but applauds
when the downed player walks off or is
assisted off the field.

———

He does not boo his own team, no
matter how inept their play or how many
times they have broken his heart.

———

He does not say bad things to
or about spectators who are rooting
for the other team, and does not
gloat if his team wins.

———

He does not knock anyone over while
racing to get a foul or home run into the
stands, or grapple fiercely with others over
T-shirt or candy-bar giveaways.

———

He sits in his seat on his bottom,
not on his knees or feet, or perch on the
armrest so as not to block the view of
those behind him.

———

He does not make untoward
remarks—"That's stupid; I could have
painted that!"—about the art he is viewing
in a museum or gallery. The audio tour of
the exhibit might be enthusiastically
received by children accustomed
to Walkmans.

———

He only takes the books he can read
during a visit to the library, then takes
them to the book cart when he is done.

———

He takes turns on the computers
at the library.

PARENT POINTERS

Do not force cultural expeditions
on your son until he is ready to sit still
for the duration.

_____

Educate your son about the respect due
performers and fellow audience members.

_____

Before entering a theatre, turn off your
beepers and cell phones or leave
them in the car.

_____

Make sure bathroom needs are attended to
before being seated, and check to be sure
chewing gum has been disposed of properly.

_____

Lead the way to the seat.

_____

Carry a cough drop or throat lozenge
in case the need arises; if an
uncontrollable coughing fit begins,
leave the seats for the lobby as
unobtrusively and quickly as possible.

―――――

Take out of the theater what you
brought into the theater.

―――――

Never take small children to movies
that are clearly intended for adults,
whether by virtue of their rating or the
sophistication of their content. If you
cannot retain a baby-sitter, wait for
another night or rent the video.

―――――

Do not get into an argument with another
audience member over his bad behavior or
a spectator at a sporting event for smoking
or being intoxicated; inform an usher and
he or she will take care of it.

―――――

Exhibit good sportsmanship at sporting events, resisting the urge to point out the shortstop's shortcomings, boo bad plays, get into an argument with a fan of the opposing team, or drink too much beer.

_____

Be aware of and versed in the more stringent rules of watching a golf game or tennis match.

TRY THIS AT HOME

Before attending a play, an opera, or a symphony concert with your son, spend a few moments at home discussing the plot or the composer. Give him a brief outline of the play or the story behind the opera (particularly if it will be sung in another language), the sections of the orchestra, and the conductor's job. A little bit of education opens a window, and an informed viewer or listener is a more interested one.

Before going to a sporting event, read the sports pages together and check where the teams are in the standings, identify each team's leaders and what type of rivalry might exist between the opponents.

SOME GOOD ADVICE

When taking a young gentleman to the theater for the first time, you might want to commit to just one half of the event. That way the boy knows that if he hates it, he can leave at intermission, but if everything is going well, he can stay for the remainder of the performance.

Expose your son to museums in small, graduated doses; do not force a child or young man to endure hours of European Portraiture or Early American farming implements. An afternoon at Cooperstown might be more enjoyable all the way around.

Chapter Ten

TRAVELING MANNERS

Just a few generations ago, families nearly always traveled together by automobile. As long as the eventual destination was reachable by some combination of blacktop, gravel, and dirt road, then a car was the way to go.

Hidden from view of anyone outside of the immediate family, packed in the back seat of the car, children were free—as free as their parents allowed them—to be as obnoxious and unruly as anyone would be after four hours in a confined space. In my personal experience, this bad behavior included everything from pinching, poking, punching, and name-calling to what my mother was convinced was deliberate car sickness just to get my father to pull over and let us out. As my mother carried all food and beverage necessities on board, the only reason to stop was for gas. Until then, we were expected to "hold it." On one memorable trip my vows of pending and disastrous car sickness went unheeded right up until the moment I leaned over and threw up all over my little sister, who was seated in the middle of the front seat between my parents. After that incident we made fairly regular stops en route, once every two or three hours anyway. It was during one of those stops that we somehow forgot my brother; five kids got out of the car, and four kids got back in. We were a good half-hour down the road before someone noticed Jimmy wasn't in the car, though for a few minutes more, my mother was convinced he was hiding under the beach towels. When we got back to the rest stop, there was my brother, sitting on a high stool behind the information counter like a king on a throne, wearing the highway patrolman's hat, drinking a soda, and eating a candy bar. The rest of us were insanely jealous, which made my mother all the more vigilant during rest stops, determined that no one would get away with a stunt like that again.

The skyrocketing cost of gasoline, coinciding with the deregulation of the airline industry and Americans' fundamental desire to do everything faster, changed all of that. I was nineteen the first time I got on an airplane; my children both reached that milestone before their first birthdays. Before I had children of my own, I greeted the sight of a mother carrying a baby or hauling children down the aisle of a plane with the same dread that I would a root canal.

Of course the trials and tribulations of motherhood have since imbued me with unshakable compassion for all parents traveling with small children, but not so much that I would patiently tolerate rude behavior from a child or inattentive or indifferent supervision from an attending adult. In such confined space it is crucial that parents strictly enforce courteous behavior from their children.

The advent of more affordable airfare has had the unfortunate side effect of introducing a more casual approach to air travel. I am not lobbying for a return to the days of suit and tie, hats, and gloves, but I would sooner sit three hours beside a screaming, wailing infant than three minutes beside a hirsute man in shorts, sandals, and a tank top who has mistaken his powerful body odor for irresistible pheromones that will result in a date with the cute blonde flight attendant. If a young man is dressed like he is going to the beach, he will likely act as though he were at the beach. When a young gentleman travels by plane, he dresses neatly in school clothes.

A young gentleman follows all instructions when boarding, never jumping into line before his time. He assists his beleaguered parents by carrying his own bags. While maneuvering the slim aisle of an aircraft, a young gentleman is aware of other passengers trying to maneuver their carry-on bags overhead or under their seats. He does not, though he is smaller, squeeze past them but waits, and if he is of sufficient size, he offers to help. Once at his row he gathers and stows those things he has brought to occupy him on the flight and quickly takes his seat to allow other passengers to pass. If another passenger comes along to occupy the vacant window seat, a young gentleman gets up to let that person pass.

While some airlines have recently widened the seat cushion and added more knee room, the fact remains that every passenger, no matter his size, is allotted about two square feet of space. A young gentleman does not sprawl in his seat but keeps his knees no more than a couple of inches apart. Most airline seats can be moved to a reclining position. It is considerate to ask the person behind you if they mind you reclining the seat. As there is little difference in the two positions (reclined and upright), a young gentleman shouldn't need to recline the seat anyway. And a young gentleman never kicks the back of the seat in front of him.

A young gentleman responds politely when spoken to by a fellow passenger, but by opening a book or putting on headphones, he can signal that he would prefer not to carry on a lengthy conversation about his grades and extracurricular habits. A young man does not call the harried flight attendant for frivolous matters, nor does he ask the flight attendant to recite the beverage menu, bring him more ice, or exchange his turkey sandwich for ham. He does not ask a fellow passenger if he is going to eat his cookie. A young gentleman turns off the volume on his computer and wears headphones if he is playing Game Boy. If he is listening to CDs on a Walkman, he does not turn the volume up loud enough for seatmates to hear, nor does he sing along with the music.

When the plane lands, a young gentleman resists the urge to imitate fellow passengers who do not believe rules apply to them but remains seated until the plane is secured at the gate and the seat belt sign is turned off. He retrieves his carry-ons as efficiently as possible and offers to help other passengers if he is able. At the luggage carousel, a young gentleman does not push in front of others to get his bag.

Rules of air travel generally apply to other modes of long-distance transportation such as trains and buses.

When staying at a hotel, a young gentleman remembers that he is not the only guest. He does not treat the lobby as a gymnasium or ride up and down in the glass elevator as if it were an amusement park ride. When boarding an elevator, he waits until all disembarking passengers exit, then he moves as far to the back as possible after pushing the button for his floor. If he is closest to the control panel, he might hold the doors for others to get in safely and ask them what floor they would like. He does not punch all the buttons on an elevator or push the alarm or emergency stop button to see what will happen. He does not talk on the elevator emergency phone.

In his room he remembers that there are other guests beside, above, and below him. He does not jump on the bed; turn the television or radio up exceedingly loud; bounce a ball off the floor, ceiling, or walls; slam drawers and doors; or roughhouse with his siblings.

When riding in a taxi, a young gentleman gets in first and slides across the seat, saving less agile adults the trouble. He allows the adult to give the driver their destination, and does not make fun of the driver's accent or name posted on his license. He takes his belongings out of the cab when they reach their destination.

When taking public transportation, a young gentleman has his token or fare ready at the turnstile or door of the bus so as not to delay other riders. He takes a seat if one is available; if one is not, he finds a way to secure his position so that sudden movements do not send him flying into another rider's lap. If he has a seat on a full bus, and an elderly person or a woman with small children boards, a young gentleman gets up and offers his seat. When his stop is imminent, a young man prepares to disembark and moves through the mass without shoving, saying "Excuse me" as needed.

When going through a door, a young gentleman makes sure not to allow the door to slam on the person behind him. Instead, he holds it open for that person to catch. If he is strong enough, a young gentleman can open the door for others and let them pass through. A young gentleman does not play in revolving doors or stop them to trap a sibling or friend inside. He does not push them around so quickly that someone might get hurt.

You Know You Are Raising A Gentleman If . . .

He presents a neat appearance and maintains control of his belongings when traveling.

He makes correct use of the pillows and
blanket offered by the flight attendant,
and does not confuse his seat for a bed.

————

He does not try repeatedly to open a
bathroom door that is clearly occupied in
an attempt to hurry the occupant.

————

He leaves the lavatory in better condition
than he found it.

————

He does not bring messy foods
or ones with very strong odors
on board a plane.

————

He keeps the volume of his Walkman at a
level only he can hear, and turns it off
during take-off or landing.

————

He turns off the volume on his computer
and Game Boy games.

————

PARENT POINTERS

Present a neat appearance and maintain
control of your belongings.

————

Do all you can to be certain your own
children are sitting with you and not the
nice elderly lady ten rows back.

————

Do not bury your head in a
book and tune out your son; he is your
responsibility. The flight attendant
is not a baby-sitter.

————

Bring along compact diversions for
small boys, and allow an older boy to
pack his own backpack.

————

Do not assume that a boy under the age of
eight can master the intricacies of an
airplane bathroom by himself.

————

Present a good example to your children
by following air industry policies and
regulations, no matter how frustrated you
may be by canceled flights, lost luggage,
and snippy personnel.

———

Do not succumb to horn
blowing, ranting, vulgar physical
gestures, or other unmistakable signs
of road rage in the car.

———

Instruct your son to stand up and offer his
seat on a crowded bus or subway.

———

Always open doors for the elderly
and mothers pushing strollers
or carrying babies.

Try This At Home

If your son is going to be flying solo—to
visit a grandparent or a non-custodial parent—
you must thoroughly prepare him beforehand.

Tell him what will be expected of him, and go over all of the above rules of mannerly travel. Be sure he knows that while rules of talking to strangers are relaxed on an airplane, if a fellow passenger says or does anything inappropriate to him or makes him uncomfortable in any way, he should get up from his seat and privately inform a flight attendant immediately. He should never go with anyone who has not been pre-authorized by you, even if that person says you have sent them. Most airlines prohibit children twelve and under from anything but non-stop flights.

SOME GOOD ADVICE

On a flight from Dallas to Gunnison, Colorado, bad weather forced our landing in Colorado Springs instead. We sat on the runway for *five* hours before flying back to Dallas. The flight, like many these days, didn't provide a meal. People were famished, a condition that in addition to the stale air, the confined space, and the lengthy delay, led to extreme crankiness. One mother had packed boxes of raisins and some granola bars in a bag for her own three children, and she generously shared with two other children on board. Another passenger contributed some chewing gum to the kids, and another had Lifesavers, so they were content for a good portion of the time. In these days of delays and cancellations, never board a flight without a supply of snacks for your kids (or extra diapers if you are still using them). A flight that starts out as an hour could easily be stretched to four or five, and not only will your kids be happier if you are prepared, but your fellow passengers will be grateful.

Chapter Eleven

WHEN NATURE CALLS: BATHROOMS, BELCHING, BOOGERS, GAS, SPITTING, AND SCRATCHING

From time to time, nature calls on all of us to attend to certain needs. Nowhere is the great divide between the genders more evident than in how each sex attends to these needs.

Generally, girls treat such needs privately and even consider them a little bit embarrassing, while boys regard them as a reason for public celebration. A young girl may very well be capable of belching the alphabet, but rarely do we witness one showing off that particular talent in public. Think of the mayhem that would ensue at Junior Miss Pageants if that were the case.

On the other hand, a boy who has mastered this stupid human trick is much admired by other boys. I know this because my son is one of those boys, something I discovered while driving him and two of his friends to a baseball game (where they could observe two more particularly masculine skills: spitting and scratching). Belching the alphabet is not my son's only gift; he can also make loud noises under his arm *and* under his knee.

There is no argument that children's television and movies have become more vulgar, with a disturbing inclination towards bathroom humor. Once they reach adolescence, boys can avail themselves of a questionable entertainment genre entirely devoted to gross-out humor.

Even without exposure to wide-screen glorification of what is better carried out behind closed doors—or at least with some discretion—young boys will find all "bathroom" words infinitely amusing and irrationally hilarious. It's annoying but not alarming. Belching and passing gas are also natural, and a young boy should never be shamed for the act itself.

If a young gentleman has mastered the art of belching the alphabet, there is no way he is not going to show off that achievement to his friends. He does not, however, perform the stunt in a classroom, a place of worship, a restaurant, a party, his parent's office, for his grandmother's bridge club, or anywhere else people may be offended. In other words, belching the alphabet should be an exclusive and command performance open only to a select few, in very private locations.

If a young man accidentally belches or passes gas in public or in a small group, the mild offense can be resolved by simply saying, "Excuse me"; no elaboration is necessary. If someone else passes gas or belches, a young gentleman does not laugh uproariously, point fingers, one-up the offender, or make crude remarks. If a young gentleman knows he is going to belch, he keeps his lips closed to prevent a cacophonous expulsion and if he feels the dire need to pass gas, a young gentleman can excuse himself to a bathroom or an area far enough away from his company to spare them discomfort.

There is no doubt that boys have more fun learning to pee in the toilet than girls; every time is like target practice. Still, young men should keep something in mind: someone has to clean the toilet, and since it typically is not him, the courteous thing to do is keep his urine where it belongs—in the toilet bowl. When using a bathroom that is not equipped with a urinal, a boy puts the seat up before urinating and back down when he is finished. If he still gets the seat wet, he should wipe it off with a piece of toilet paper.

When a young gentleman uses a toilet, he closes the door to the stall, flushes after use, then washes his hands. He uses a towel rather than the seat of his pants for drying and places the towel back where he found it or puts discarded paper towels in the trash; the general vicinity of the trash can does not count.

For completely inexplicable reasons, many

very young children get into the habit of not only picking their noses but tasting the contents. This should be discouraged early and often. Everyone at one time or another feels the need to remove something from his nose. Even in private it is a good idea for a young man to get into the habit of executing this with discretion or using a tissue to explore the inner reaches.

Scratching and spitting are two habits of questionable taste that are also nearly always the exclusive domain of the male gender. Both seem to have something to do with professional athletes. They not only engage in these practices regularly but often on television and the Jumbotron with little regard for modesty or decorum. Being generous I might theorize that the reason for scratching has to do with the protective and support equipment athletes must wear. Spitting is obviously the only effective method for getting rid of noxious chewing tobacco juice or the hulls of sunflower seeds. Even so these on-field habits nearly always travel off-field as well. Young boys naturally emulate professional athletes, and even the ones who are years away from using protective gear or chewing tobacco will imitate their heroes. It is certainly a parent's responsibility in teaching good manners to ask for more discretion when attending to itches and insist on no unnecessary or exhibition spitting in public.

You Know You Are Raising A Gentleman If . . .

He squelches his belches in public and leaves the room if he feels the need to pass gas. He should say, "Excuse me," if he should unexpectedly or unavoidably do either in the company of others.

———

He employs accurate aim towards toilet bowls. If an accident occurs, he wipes the seat but does not put paper towels in the toilet.

———

He puts the seat down after use.

_____

He cleans out the sink after use.

_____

He uses a small amount of air freshener if
one is available when his visit to the
bathroom results in a lingering odor.

_____

He does not glorify his own
personal habits, nor call attention
to those of others.

_____

He uses a tissue or handkerchief
with utmost discretion to clear his nose
of annoying obstructions.

_____

He does not treat spitting as
a competitive sport but as a means
to rid himself of excess nasal drip, and
then only with certainty as to the
targeted receptacle.

_____

He does not scratch his groin
in view of others, but instead
he turns his back.

PARENT POINTERS

Employ the same good personal habits
you seek from your son.

————

Do not engage in immature
competitions with your son as they
encourage lewd behavior.

————

Make your son aware that the
bathroom is a room where privacy
must be respected.

————

Respect your son's privacy unless there
is obvious distress or some imminent
danger involved.

————

Be aware of the vulgar nature of some children's programming and make informed decisions about what type of humor to which you are exposing your child.

―――

Do not laugh at belching and farting.

―――

Do not laugh at, nor appear too horrified by, your son's ability to belch "Happy Birthday," but impress upon him the rudeness of doing it in public.

―――

Try This At Home

Leaving the room, or at least the dinner table, is what a young man should do if he knows he needs to pass gas. If he is in his classroom, church, a restaurant, or an airplane, he can excuse himself to go to the bathroom. But what if he is in a car? It would be impractical and silly to pull over every time he needs to pass gas. Instead, in our car, my children issue a warning. When one of them says, "Safety," we all roll down our window.

Some Good Advice

One of my friends has two boys. She told me she toilet trained the first one just before he turned three during the summer at the beach. She simply allowed him to pee outside: against a tree in their yard, on a sand dune, or even into the bay from their pier. She said he enjoyed the alfresco urinating experience so much that he was soon out of diapers altogether. My friend thought this was wonderful until they went back to the city. They weren't there five minutes before her son was peeing on a tree in the middle of a busy sidewalk. It took months to break him of his habit of urinating au naturale. The moral of the story: potty training isn't called *potty* training for nothing. Unless you're lost in the woods, pee and poop go in the toilet, and that goes for grown-up boys as well.

Chapter Twelve

TEMPER TEMPER

According to child development experts, for children aged one to three, temper tantrums are a natural and predictable expression of a child's first surges of independence. It's how parents react to these early immature and usually very embarrassing expressions of frustration that may determine how their son learns to manage his anger in the future.

During one of our first annual Easter egg hunts, when the oldest children were still toddlers, a three-year-old boy looked in his basket and determined that he had not gotten as many eggs as he thought he deserved, though certainly no less than most of the other children. His reaction to this deprivation was to hurl himself onto the ground and throw an ear-splitting, wailing, bawling, screaming, crying, kicking, flailing fit—one of the worst ever witnessed by any parent on hand that day. The other children stared in wide-eyed, open-mouthed amazement as his face turned redder and redder and his wailing louder and louder. Many of the parents also stared in amazement as the child's parents kneeled beside him desperately trying to appease him, promising that if he would just stop they would get him as many eggs and as much candy as he wanted. It took some time for the child to hear their supplications over his own shrieking, but eventually he quieted down and, still sniffling, accepted their offers of appeasement. A few feet away from the spectacle, some of us predicted trouble down the road.

Fast forward a few years to Halloween night. The child was eight years old and out trick-or-treating with several other children and their parents. The child dilly-dallied, inspecting each piece of candy that he got. In an attempt to keep pace with the group, his mother decided to skip a couple of houses on the route so they could catch up with everyone else. Suddenly, a screeching howl pierced the air. The Monster Child found that proposal completely unacceptable and expressed his disapproval by throwing another ear-splitting, wailing, bawling, screaming, crying, kicking, flailing fit. The child was old enough to talk and threw in some scathing insults along with a few "I hate you's" for good measure. As the mother attempted to placate him, the father walked away in disgust but not without a pointed barb of his own: "*You've* made him this way, now *you* do something with him!" A few feet away from the spectacle, some of us predicted a fortune in therapy.

What is wrong with this picture? Plenty. First, while every parent can expect a temper tantrum from their two and three year old, giving in to the child is the worst possible method of quelling the storm—at least if you don't want to endure years and years of volcanic eruptions. When a boy under the age of three has a temper tantrum, a parent remains calm and walks away. If the tantrum takes place in public—as many do—the parent picks up the child and leaves the party, the store, the restaurant, or whatever location until the boy regains control. After the boy regains control, the parent can hold the child, explaining that although being two can be frustrating, throwing a fit—as they say in the South—will not result in the desired objective.

A very young child should not be punished for what is truly a natural expression, but he should not be rewarded either. After the child turns three, a parent must let the son know in no uncertain terms that temper tantrums will not be tolerated and that not only will the child not get what he is ranting about, but that his uncontrollable behavior will result in some type of retribution. Just as a parent helps a child learn to recite the alphabet, sing a song, and ride a bicycle, a parent is responsible—through word and deed—for teaching a son how to control his temper, handle his frustrations, and express his anger in a mature and socially acceptable manner.

A young gentleman, no matter how angry he is that he lost a video game, does not respond by smashing the keyboard or throwing the Game Boy across the room. A young gentleman, no matter how upset he is that he did not get the Nikes that he wanted, does not respond by deliberately trashing the shoes that his parents have bought him. A young gentleman, no matter how affronted he is when a classmate cuts in front of him in the cafeteria line, does not respond by pushing or poking. A young gentleman, no matter how frustrated he is for striking out, does not hurl his bat and slam his batting helmet in the dugout.

The measure of a mature person is how they react to challenging and difficult situations. When I was barely twenty-one, I prepared an impressive dinner for my boyfriend, who happened to be a gourmet chef. While he was in another room of the apartment practicing kicks and thrusts for his black belt in karate, I was in the kitchen cooking away. Finally, after a full afternoon of hard work, I set the food on the table and announced that dinner was ready. From the other room came the sounds of grunting and repeated contact with a mat fastened to the wall. I called him again and again. Finally, he emerged panting, sweaty, and shirtless, and sat down at the table. I was so angry at his cavalier approach to my generous outpouring of love and devotion that I picked up the roast chicken off the platter and heaved it at him, along with a few choice words. He ducked, and the chicken slapped against the wall, splattering his bare back with hot chicken drippings before slowly sliding down the wall to the floor, where it remained until much later that evening. To his credit (and thanks to his keenly advanced maturity level), he simply got up and retreated to the back room, where he resumed his karate workout. I was so horrified by my overreaction to what was basically discourteous behavior that I picked up my glass and bottle of wine and retreated to the patio where I stayed until I cooled down and could make amends for hurling a hot chicken at his head.

The point is that every person, young and old, will sometimes engage in impetuous behavior that he or she will later have cause to regret. An apology takes just a moment, but hastens forgiveness and has a lasting effect on relationships. If a young man loses his temper and, in expressing his anger, does or says something that hurts another, he first allows himself a moment to cool down, then offers a sincere, in-person apology whenever possible. If face-to-face contact is not possible, then telephoned or written amends can be substituted. If, in his anger, his actions result in something being damaged or broken, his apology must be accompanied by an offer to make reparations.

A young man learns this because he sees his parents apologize when they lose their tempers or say angry, hurtful words. He learns this because when his parents see that their son is losing control, they intervene. He learns this because when he does lose control, his parents insist he apologize; until he does, he will remain in his room.

You Know You Are Raising A Gentleman If . . .

He does not express anger, disappointment, or frustration by using bad language or insulting someone.

_____

He does not express anger, disappointment, or frustration by throwing, kicking, punching, or breaking something.

_____

He apologizes as soon as possible when he loses control.

_____

He does not shout to get someone's attention.

_____

He never uses words like "fatso," "stupid," "butthead," "idiot," "porky," "retard," or "faggot" when addressing another.

Parent Pointers

Do not respond to a temper tantrum by giving in to a child's tantrum or promising to get him a treat if he stops.

_____

If your son is having a temper tantrum in a public place or around other people, take him to another room or outside.

_____

Do not react to your son's bad behavior with similar bad behavior, such as hitting a child to stop him from hitting.

_____

Do your best not to raise your voice in anger to a child, unless a child is in danger.

_____

Do not yell at other people or question their parenting in front of their children.

———

Do not call other people names. Even if you think the driver who just made a left turn from the far right lane is an idiot, you are only stating the obvious if you announce it.

———

If you curse or use vulgarities in front of your children, don't be surprised when they begin using the same words. It sounds just as bad coming from your mouth as it does from theirs.

———

Do not throw golf clubs, tennis rackets, bats, lamps, jewelry, chickens, or anything else in anger.

———

If you lose your temper with your child, apologize.

———

Accept apologies quickly and graciously
when they are made to you.

Part of forgiving is forgetting. Once
someone apologizes and you accept the
apology, it is over. Let it go.

TRY THIS AT HOME

When I became a mom, I made a conscious
effort to stop cursing, especially around the
children, but it happens. Sometimes I'm not
even aware of it myself. They may overhear me
on the telephone or in a conversation with a
friend, and they are quick to point out my
infraction. We have a "fine" jar, and every time I
use a curse word, I have to deposit a quarter.
Similarly, if my children tell someone to shut
up, or call someone stupid, they are fined as
well. Once a year, we use the change for a good
cause, such as buying books or toys for a family
shelter or domestic violence center or adopting
a needy family at Christmas. The rule is that

you cannot use the money collected from your bad behavior to reward yourself.

Some Good Advice

My mother was a stay-at-home mom with five children. When the oldest was nine, the youngest was born. She had a herd to ride herd on and plenty of opportunities for discipline. I was often the recipient of her fierce attention, but every time she was forced to have words with me, she did it privately. I do not recall my mother ever admonishing or punishing us in public or in front of our friends. There were times, if my behavior was extreme, that she sent my friends home, so that she could send me to my room, but she did it in a very simple way: "Mary, we're glad you came to play, but Kay needs some time by herself. We'll see you tomorrow." Avoid disciplining your child in public or in front of anyone else.

Chapter Thirteen

SEX, RELIGION, POLITICS, AND SANTA CLAUS

The cardinal rule of convivial dinner parties is to avoid discussing sex, religion, or politics. That may be true, but if you ask me, it could make for a pretty dull evening. Surely mature adults can be counted upon to engage in thoughtful discourse on stimulating and controversial topics with respect and regard for opinions that differ from their own.

In reality, since otherwise mature adults are not always capable of this, we can hardly expect it of our children. Does that mean that in order to be mannerly subjects that may spark disagreement must be avoided? Not necessarily, but boys should be taught that opinions are like noses: everybody has one, but none of them are exactly the same. Just because somebody's opinion is different doesn't make them wrong or stupid or idiotic.

In most parts of the world it is considered bad manners to ask someone what their religious affiliation is or where they attend church. In the South it is perfectly natural in the course of casual conversation for a new acquaintance to inquire, "Where do you go to church?" For many people in the South going to church is as much social as it is religious. (It's not called the Bible Belt for nothing.) A young man might, out of curiosity, ask his new friend where he attends church, but he does not make a negative comment in response. A young Methodist gentleman does not accuse his Catholic friend of worshipping idols, nor does a conservative Christian gentleman warn his Jewish classmate that he is going straight to hell.

A young man may invite a friend to attend church or temple with him. He does not insist that his friend participate in any part of the service that is not comfortable to him. Likewise, if a young man attends church or temple with a friend of a different religious persuasion, he is respectful of the service and practices, but he is not required to participate in communion, testimony, laying on of hands, or even singing.

In situations where a public prayer is said, a young gentleman who does not subscribe to the theology of the assembled does not make a display of his differences but shows respect by remaining quiet through the prayer. If grace is said before a meal at which he is a guest, he does not announce that his family does not say grace but simply bows his head.

The 2000 presidential campaign was protracted and contentious. Thus it was a wonderful opportunity for parents and teachers to offer children valuable lessons in fairness, civic responsibility, and respect for people of differing opinions and stances. Thanks to the endless news coverage of even the most mundane details, children were exposed to relentless sparring from both parties, good and bad. My children were insatiably curious about the process, the players, and their politics. I thought this was a good thing. What was not a good thing was the name-calling that sometimes ensued.

Unless someone is wearing a T-shirt, hat, or pin announcing their candidate, a young gentleman does not ask someone for whom they are voting. Many schools participate in a program called Kids Vote, which allows children to register their choice of candidates. When children ask other kids for whom they voted, what they are really asking is: "Who are your parents supporting?" A young gentleman does not mock another child's choice or political affiliation or make disparaging comments about his or her candidate. He does not accuse the other candidate of cheating in order to win, nor does he gloat if his candidate wins.

If a boy holds strong beliefs about a subject—from the designated hitter rule to global warming or capital punishment—he does not try to impose his beliefs on others, nor make fun of those whose beliefs differ from his own. He may express his thoughts on the topic if he can do so in a non-confrontational and non-contentious manner.

An even more treacherous territory is sex, sex education, sexual abuse, sexual harassment, and sexual proclivities. There are countless books devoted to this subject; this book is not one of them.

When my son was about five years old, he simultaneously discovered my Victoria's Secret catalog, and the effect photos of near-naked women can have on a young man's sexual organ—something he pointed out to his sister and me. While I assured him that the reaction was perfectly normal, I took the opportunity to tell him that it was not an achievement that should be displayed to others. While a mother can and should talk to her son about sex, this is an ideal time for a father to have a talk with his son about sex, love, physicality, personal habits, and respect for women.

A young gentleman does not exhibit his

private parts to others, nor does he show off a state of arousal. He does his own sexual exploration in the privacy of his bedroom or bathroom and does not share his discoveries with others. If the boy is following those guidelines and is accidentally discovered by a parent when he is engaged in sexual exploration, a parent does not make the boy feel ashamed of what he is doing. (He should be stopped if he is doing something physically or hygienically harmful.)

A young gentleman does not touch other children—boys or girls—on their private parts or ask them to touch his. This is not just good manners; in these hyper-sensitive and highly litigious times, it is a good precaution against legal charges or lawsuits.

Children are sexually curious and exploratory. Parents should discuss with their pediatrician the best time and manner to educate their children on sexuality. When, how much, and in what way parents deal with the sexual education and maturation of their children is entirely personal and individual. When boys begin sharing their knowledge and growing awareness of their sexuality with others, manners and courtesy really come into play.

Young boys often disguise or assimilate their curiosity and growing awareness of sexuality and changing bodies with humor. For some time I could not say the words *nuts* or *balls*, or the name Dick to my boys without them exploding in gales of laughter. No matter what, young boys are going to say these words to other young boys. It is important to teach a young man the correct word for sexual organs and the correct time and place to use such words.

Finally, on the subject of Santa Claus, the Tooth Fairy and the Easter Bunny: when a young gentleman discovers or is told the truth about these childhood fantasies, he should not share this with other children who may still be captivated by their magic. Soon after his eighth Christmas, my son came to me and asked, with a fair degree of trepidation, if Santa Claus was real. I responded in the time-honored parental response to tough questions: "What do you think?" He, rather wistfully and somewhat hopeful of a positive response, said, "I don't think he is." It was all I could do not to burst into tears, but as he was on the verge himself, I very gently replied, "Do you mean that you don't believe there is a jolly fat man who lives on the North Pole with Mrs. Claus and hundreds of little elf helpers who make millions of toys all year long, then pack them into a little sleigh that is pulled by eight tiny reindeer to deliver all those presents in a single night to good boys and girls all over the world?" Even he had to laugh at the image, which helped diffuse the disappointment. I told him that believing in Santa Claus was a wonderful, magical thing that children and their parents loved to celebrate for as long as possible. I also asked him to remember the true meaning of Christmas.

He nodded his head solemnly then asked the Big Question: "Does this mean I won't get any presents anymore?" After I assured him that he would still get presents under the tree and a stocking by the fireplace as long as he wanted, his next concern was keeping it a secret from his sister, who happens to be two years older than him, and had known for nearly that long the truth about Santa Claus. I pointed out to him how generous it had been of her to help me keep that fantasy alive for him until he discovered the truth himself, and that he was now charged with that same responsibility when it came to children younger than him. He walked away from the conversation feeling very happy. I closed my office door and shed a few tears for one more piece of his childhood gone forever.

YOU KNOW YOU ARE RAISING A GENTLEMAN IF . . .

He does not make fun of or pass judgment on another person's religious beliefs or practices.

———

He is respectful when
attending a religious service with a
friend of a different theology.

_____

He does not ask a person for whom
he or she is voting.

_____

He does not make fun of
another person's political affiliation,
policies, or candidates.

_____

He does not impose his spiritual or
political beliefs on others.

_____

He does not use locker room words
in inappropriate places.

_____

He does not leer at girls or women, or
make offensive and inappropriate remarks
about their looks or bodies.

PARENT POINTERS

Do not make comments or pass judgment in front of your children about another's spiritual or political beliefs.

———

Do not make a guest in your home or place of worship engage in practices that are uncomfortable for him.

———

Do not say horrid things about politicians or community leaders.

———

Do not call elected officials names; whether you voted for the President of the United States or not, he (perhaps one day, she) is still the president of the country, an office deserving much respect.

———

Make every effort to sexually educate your son in a timely and unthreatening fashion.

———

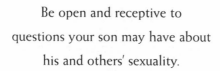

Be open and receptive to
questions your son may have about
his and others' sexuality.

―――

Do not make up answers to those
questions, or pass on false information.

―――

Use the appropriate words for sexual
organs, reproduction, and sexual acts.

―――

Do not make inappropriate,
leering, or derogatory remarks about
other people's bodies.

TRY THIS AT HOME

I am a rabid voter. Voting is more than a right;
it's a responsibility of every American. I vote in
every election, from school board to presidential,
and since my children have been babies, I have
taken them to the polls with me, pulling their
strollers into the voting booth. As soon as they
were old enough to reach, I let them push the

buttons and pull the lever. Now that they are reading, we look over the sample ballot in the newspaper before election day, and I wait until they are home from school so they can come with me. They look forward to it and even more to the day when they can vote themselves. As we saw in the 2000 election, every vote *does* count.

SOME GOOD ADVICE

Don't tell your children more than they want to know or are ready to hear. When your four year old asks where babies come from, he is not asking for a lesson on reproduction and sexual intercourse. He is asking a simple question which only requires a simple answer: "Babies grow in a special place inside the mother." As he has seen pregnant women, or may be asking because his mother is looking like she swallowed a basketball, this answer will satisfy him for the time being. Do not lie to your child by telling him the stork brings babies. As he gets older, his questions will become more complicated: How does the baby get in there? How does the baby get out? Though we all believe that the birds-and-bees conversation is going to happen in some quiet, thoughtful, sharing way, the truth is that kids usually ask these questions at the most inconvenient times: in the car, at the grocery store, when you are on the phone. To them, it is just a subject they are curious about, like, "How do planes fly?" or "How do cell phones work?" Try to answer their questions, when they ask, in a truthful, straightforward, natural way, but if the subject makes you uncomfortable, or embarrassed, or you don't know how to answer, ask your pediatrician to recommend a book to help you out.

Chapter Fourteen

TELEPHONE MANNERS

Look in any playroom, pre-school or day care center and you will probably find a toy phone. Children love to imitate their parents by playing telephone, making a game of picking up the receiver, punching buttons, and babbling away in an imaginary conversation. But in every child's life there comes a time when he or she must be taught the difference between a toy telephone and the real deal. The telephone may be the best and most efficient way to reach out and touch someone, but since it provides easy access to people's homes and lives, it has a reputation as one of modern times' most irritatingly misused forms of communication.

With the exception of knowing how, when, and why to dial 911, a child should not be permitted to answer the phone or place calls until he knows how to do it properly. It is also important that your child is articulate enough that he can be understood by the caller or callee and can accurately take a message in the event the parent is unavailable. Fortunately, instructions for proper use of the telephone are fairly simple and can even be rehearsed on their toy telephone.

A young gentleman answers the telephone in his own home in one of the following ways: "Hello," "Hello, Carter residence, Martin speaking," or "Carter residence, this is Martin." He then waits for the caller to make the next move, in which case the caller will say something like, "Hello, Martin, this is Mrs. West; may I speak with your mother, please?" Depending on the circumstances, Martin might say, "I'm sorry, she isn't available right now. May I take a message?" or "Just a moment, please." A young gentleman would then—this is *very* important—either put the receiver down and find his mother or cover the receiver with his hand and call his mother to the phone. He does not yell "Mooooooooooooom!" into the telephone.

If his parents are not at home, he does not announce the absence of an adult. Instead, he says, "She is not able to come to the phone," and offers to take a message. Phones should have a pad of paper and writing implement nearby. A young gentleman takes the caller's name and a number where the caller can be reached; he writes the information legibly on the pad.

When a young gentleman places a call from his home phone, he speaks clearly and loudly enough to be heard: "Hello, this is Marshall. May I speak to Malcolm, please?" If Malcolm is not available or not at home, a young gentleman then says, "Would you please ask him to call Marshall? My number is 234-5678. Thank you."

A young man is prepared to speak to an answering machine, as most homes are now equipped with them. When a phone is answered by machine or voice mail, a young man speaks clearly, audibly, and slowly. Make the message short. "Hello, this is Marshall. Please have Malcolm call me at 234-5678. Thank you."

Answering machines are designed to take messages. Overly cute but barely decipherable outgoing messages that cause people to hang up defeat the purpose of the machine. Unless your child can articulate the greeting on your answering machine, leave it to an adult or a computer. If your child can clearly say something like, "This is 798-1700; please leave a message," without giggling, he is ready to record the outgoing announcement.

A young gentleman does not monopolize the home's only telephone line; time limits can be set on children's phone calls. If a home phone is equipped with call waiting, a child knows how to operate it. If he is on the phone when another call beeps in, he defers to the incoming call, lest it be his parent's boss calling to tell him that he will be fired unless the presentation is ready by noon tomorrow. When another call beeps into his, he says, "Please hold on a moment." He takes the next call; if it is for one of his parents, he asks the incoming caller to hold for a moment, goes back to the first call, and asks if he might call back.

A young gentleman does not place phone calls during inconvenient times, such as the dinner hour, roughly 5:30–6:30 P.M. He does not call a home before 8:00 A.M. or after 8:00 P.M. on weekdays; nor before 10:00 A.M. or after 9:00 P.M. on weekends.

If a young gentleman inadvertently dials a wrong number, he does not hang up when recognizing that fact, but instead says, "I'm sorry, I must have dialed a wrong number." If he is not sure, a young man says, "Is this 234-5678?" He does not ask the person answering the phone what number he has called, and if the reverse occurs, he does not give out his telephone number to someone he doesn't know on the line.

A young gentleman is aware that cellular phones carry a high price for their convenience, and that no matter how cute they are, they are not toys. Unless he has been given permission to do so, a young gentleman does not place calls on his parents' cell phone. He does not give his parents' cell phone number to his buddies. If he is asked to make or take a call on a cell phone, he knows how to disconnect calls so that unnecessary charges do not pile up.

Many parents are equipping their children with beepers and cell phones, particularly if they are separated from their children for long periods of time. The ground rules for the use of these should be pre-set and firm. If a parent is using a beeper to keep in touch, a five-minute call-back rule might be imposed. If you have sent your son to a movie theatre or mall with a beeper, make sure he also has the correct change in his pocket to place a call on a public phone. If you are letting your child use a cell phone, you might set a rule that he is only allowed to call his parents on the cell phone, not every buddy in his eighth grade class.

Children with beepers and cell phones must know and practice proper etiquette. A young gentleman turns the devices off in movie theaters, school, or church. He shouldn't use the cell phone when his full attention is required for his safety, such as on a bicycle. Misuse of the instruments should result in their confiscation.

You Know You Are Raising A Gentleman If . . .

He speaks clearly and audibly on the telephone and knows how to take and leave a message.

———

He does not yell "Mom!" directly into the receiver when the caller has asked for his mother, nor does he chomp gum or food while on the phone.

———

He knows to turn his cellular phone off
during movies or at church or school.

———

He does not call too early in the morning
or too late at night.

———

He does not hog the telephone.

———

He does not take a phone into the
bathroom with him.

———

He does not disregard calls coming in
while he is on another, nor ignore the
original caller.

———

He returns the portable phone
to its receiver.

———

He does not answer the phone in
someone else's house.

———

He does not place a call
from someone else's house without
their permission.

———

He does not place prank
or obscene calls; besides being rude,
it is also illegal.

PARENT POINTERS

Teach your son how, when, and why
to use 911. Give him some examples
of the differences between a real
emergency (the house across the
street is on fire) and a problem
(the cat is up the tree and
can't get down).

———

Make sure your son knows his
home phone number and when it is
appropriate to share it.

———

Teach your son how to answer and place calls properly; until he has mastered the task, do not allow him to use the phone except in an emergency.

———

Teach your son how to use telephone amenities such as call-waiting and voice mail or answering machines.

———

Do not chew gum or food while on the phone.

———

Do not be rude to telephone solicitors. If you don't want to be bothered, cut them off promptly and politely and ask to have your name removed from their calling list.

———

Turn your cell phone ringer off in public places. If you must make or take a call, excuse yourself and converse privately.

———

Do not drive and talk on the cell
phone simultaneously. It is dangerous and
may be illegal.

————

Do not ask your son to lie on your behalf by
telling a caller you are not available when
you simply do not want to take the call.

Try This At Home

I don't believe in children having a television
in their bedrooms, unmonitored access to the
Internet, or their own phone lines. I think you
are asking for trouble. When I was growing up,
we had one phone in the house on the wall in
the dining room, which was where all of my
siblings did their homework, my mother wrote
letters, and my father read the paper. When I
wanted to talk to my friends, I had to stretch
the cord to the breaking point just to hear over
the din. Thanks to cordless phones, a boy today
can easily take a call privately. A phone
installed in an older boy's bedroom is fine, but

it should remain on the family line and be subject to rules of time limits and long distance by permission only.

SOME GOOD ADVICE

If you have a computer in your home and are an Internet subscriber, it would be wise to invest in a separate phone line for Internet use. By the second grade, my son was using the Internet to do research for school; it has certainly replaced the *World Book Encyclopedia* in many homes. He may spend an hour looking up frogs, their habits and habitats, but he would tie up the phone for an hour.

Our family computer is in a corner of the family room so that I can monitor what he is doing and where he is going without appearing to be policing. Learn how to use filters to block access to "adult" sites but still keep a watchful eye as filters do not work for everything.

Chapter Fifteen

STARING AND DIFFERENCES

Nearly ten years ago we moved into a house on a street in what is known as a "transitional neighborhood," one of older homes in various states of either disrepair or renovation, and extremely diverse racially, ethnically, and socioeconomically.

A friend who had spent all of his life in a rural community that consisted of one thousand residents, most of whom he knew personally, brought his truck and came to help us move. We spent much of the day carrying furniture and boxes in and out of the house, saying hello to new neighbors as they passed by or came over to introduce themselves. Finally, as dusk settled over my new street and I was admiring the sidewalks, the neat lawns and beginnings of landscaping projects, the inviting porches fronting the bungalows, Victorians and four-squares, we sat on my own front porch drinking a couple of well-deserved beers. He turned to me and said with complete innocence, "So, are you the only white people on the block?" I looked back at him and said, "No, we're not. The gay couple that lives in the yellow house, and the gay couple that lives in the blue house are also white, and the family that lives in the brick house next door to the Islamic mosque down at the end of the street are black and white. Other than that, I guess we are." He didn't say another word about it.

Parents—black, brown, white, yellow, or green—don't do their children any favors by insulating them, surrounding them only with people who look and think and act like them. Sooner or later—unless you are like my small-town friend—they will go out into the world, and it would help them immeasurably to have had exposure to and interaction with different types of people.

Parents of every race and creed teach their

children—by thought, word, and deed—that while skin color, religion, ethnic background, and sexual preference certainly contribute to who a person is, they are not *all* a person is. Making generalizations and perpetuating stereotypes about people of other races or backgrounds is wrong and ignorant. Parents also, by example, show children that bigoted remarks, slurs, and jokes will not be tolerated in their presence. By simply saying, "We do not find those types of jokes amusing" or "We are offended by that way of speaking," your child will understand the value you place on other people and hopefully follow your example. If the person making those jokes or remarks gets insulted, or persists, just walk away; do not get into an argument.

Aside from skin color and ethnic background, children will also come across people who are different from them because of physical or mental handicaps or disfigurement due to disease or accidents. A small boy can be forgiven for staring and asking awkward questions that, coming from someone older, would be extremely rude:

"Mommy, why is that man in a wheelchair?"
"Daddy, what is on that lady's face?" "Why does
that boy only have one arm?"

A parent should first tell his or her son that
he must not stare or, even worse, point at people
different from him, but that he may quietly ask
his parent a question about someone in a
wheelchair, or with a horrid facial scar, or
without an arm. If you don't know the specifics,
a good response would be to say that perhaps
the person has had an accident that put him in a
wheelchair, or that he may have suffered a
terrible burn, or that sometimes things go wrong
before babies are born so not everyone turns out
the same as everyone else. The parent also
explains that handicapped people have to work
harder than people who are not handicapped to
do things we take for granted, and that
handicapped people are proud of what they
have done to achieve a "normal" life, and they
prefer not to be treated differently from others.

A young gentleman treats handicapped

children he may know or have reason to play with as naturally as possible. A child with a handicap needs understanding, not pity. A young gentleman can assist as long as he offers first and doesn't just barge in.

If he meets someone who is deaf, a young gentleman gets his attention by lightly touching his arm or shoulder. A young man does not shout at a deaf person but speaks audibly, distinctly, and does not rush his words. Many deaf people have been taught to read lips, so a young gentleman should be certain his mouth is clearly visible.

If a young gentleman meets someone who is blind, there is no need to shout or help them get dressed, feed themselves, or move about. A young gentleman makes his entrance or departure known to a blind person. If a blind person has a guide dog, a young gentleman does not pet a Seeing Eye dog without permission, throw a ball, ask him to do tricks, or try to feed him a snack. The dog is his master's eyes, and to take him away from his job would be a disservice to both and could even be harmful.

A young gentleman does not ask a person in a wheelchair if he may drive it or take a ride. When speaking to a person in a wheelchair, a young gentleman makes every effort to have that conversation at eye level so that the person in the wheelchair does not get a crick in his neck. He does not try to assist the person in the wheelchair unless he is asked.

The mentally challenged can be frightening to children, so parents should make every effort to explain the illness or disability to their child and assure him there is nothing to fear. A young gentleman treats a mentally challenged person with compassion and respect.

YOU KNOW YOU ARE RAISING A GENTLEMAN IF . . .

He does not judge a book by its cover, or a person by the color of his skin, his religion, his clothing, house, car, or lifestyle.

———

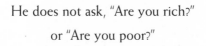

He does not ask, "Are you rich?"
or "Are you poor?"

———

He does not engage in name-calling
or disparaging jokes.

———

He does not stare or point at people
with handicaps, disabilities,
or physical defects.

———

He does not shout at physically
disabled or mentally challenged people in
an effort to be understood.

———

He does not act as if a handicap
makes a person invisible.

———

He shows kindness and
respect for the handicapped and
the challenged.

———

Parent Pointers

Never make racial or ethnic slurs, even to
repeat a story or what someone else said.

_____

Be aware of the use of words or phrases
that may be common, but are nonetheless
offensive: to Jew someone down, to
Welsh on a bet, to call someone an Indian
giver, to Gyp someone, or to call
someone a Jap.

_____

Do not repeat racist, sexist, or ethnic
jokes, or tolerate them in your presence.

_____

Do not point or stare at the handicapped.

_____

Answer your son's questions about
people different from him as simply
and clearly as possible.

_____

TRY THIS AT HOME

My cousin Billy was blind from birth. Once when we were visiting his family, Billy, who was about seven at the time, asked his mother for a glass of milk; she told him to get it himself. He got a glass from the cabinet, took the milk from the refrigerator, put the glass on the table, and put a finger inside the glass so he could measure how much he was pouring. Even so, the carton was full and he spilled a small amount on the table, something I, a fully sighted ten year old, did on a regular basis. His mother looked over and said, "For crying out loud, Billy, can't you see what you're doing?" There was dead silence for a moment, then we all laughed. Being around Billy growing up taught us not to treat him differently, and that he had gifts beyond 20/20 vision. He grew up to get a Ph.D., and traveled the world playing music in clubs and coffeehouses.

If you have a friend or acquaintance who is handicapped in some way, that person may not mind talking to your son about his or her handicap or disability, letting your son know what life is like for him or her. Answering your son's questions in an honest and forthright way would be an incredibly generous gift, and one that I don't imagine many would be reluctant to offer.

SOME GOOD ADVICE

I have a brother-in-law who is paraplegic, but he has one of those magic wheelchairs. I took him to the grocery store one day in his specially equipped van, but every single handicapped parking space was taken and remained taken for a good fifteen minutes as I circled the lot. The first one that became available was from a young woman driving a car with no handicapped tags; she had a small child with her. She looked at us a little sheepishly and said, "I'm sorry. I was just going in for a minute." Never, ever park in a handicapped parking space if you don't need one for a genuine handicap. Being in a hurry and toting small children is not a handicap. Being confined to a wheelchair is. You should be thankful that you don't need the wheelchair or the parking space.

Chapter Sixteen

PREACHERS AND TEACHERS;
CHURCH AND SCHOOL

In some Christian denominations, the first experience a child will have with formal church is his baptism, a sacred moment for family and friends. The precious baby boy dons something fancy, often an heirloom baptismal gown. Proudly the parents and godparents approach the baptismal font and hand their child to the minister. The entire congregation looks on expectantly. If he is typical of most babies, the moment the holy water is poured over his head, he will burst into a startled and piercing wail, followed by angry and vigorous crying. Everyone smiles indulgently: "Isn't that darling?"

And it is darling, but only once. After the baptism, the sound of a squalling infant or rambunctious toddler usually strikes a note of discord in the solemn sanctity of most services. Some churches deal with this issue by providing crying rooms in the back of the church where the parent on duty can retreat with the noisy babe in arms and remain included in the service, yet isolated from the other members of the congregation. Other churches and synagogues provide child care during the service, and parents are urged to take advantage of this until the maximum age limit or until such time when they feel their son is able to remain still and quiet for the hour or so required of him.

A young boy who has been entrusted to do so follows the common guidelines of courtesy while he is in church or temple. If he is not old enough to read and follow along with the order of service, a young boy brings along something *unobtrusive* to keep himself busy, the key word being unobtrusive. At a recent Easter service, my son and I were fascinated by a boy of about four who had brought along a portable garage complete with a half dozen small vehicles. He proceeded to set it up on the floor at the end of his pew and spread out nearly one foot into the aisle. There, sprawled on the floor, he ran his cars in and out of service bays, filled up at the miniature pumps, and even went so far as to make a siren noise for the police car in hot pursuit of a little red Corvette. Everyone within sight and sound of the child was appalled and thankful when an usher nipped the game in the bud. The boy began crying, and the mother, already proven to lack sound judgment and good manners, did nothing to halt the outburst, as if to say to the usher, "Now look what you've done!"

This is an extreme example of inappropriate play toys for a church but one that bears repeating, if just for its audacity. A pre-reader can bring a sticker book, a coloring book, or a sketchpad and some markers. He is not expected to do anything other than remain occupied and quiet for the duration. A young man never lies down on a pew—I once sat squarely on my son's head when he had done so—or on the floor. He may write on the bulletin but must not remove all of the printed material from the back of the pews to use as a coloring book or to make into paper airplanes.

When he is old enough, a young gentleman is encouraged to take part in those parts of the service that call for a congregation's participation. He does so with some semblance of enthusiasm and solemnity without fidgeting or slouching. If the service takes an exceptionally long time, a young gentleman may engage himself in a book or sketch pad brought along for that purpose.

A young gentleman treats his clergyperson or religion teacher with respect, using the proper title: Reverend Butcher, Dean Swanson, Father Francis, Bishop Herlong, Rabbi Kantor. If your clergyperson's habit is to stand in the back of the church following the service to greet his or her parishioners, a young gentleman stops briefly with his parents and says hello, shaking hands if the clergyperson initiates the exchange.

Long before they start kindergarten, many children have accumulated years of experience in day care, mother's day out or pre-school, and are thus somewhat prepared for the rules and regulations of educational institutions.

A young gentleman knows that the classroom is the teacher's domain, and unless he is asked to do something that goes against his religion or customs of his people, he follows the laws of the land. Though I understand that certain progressive schools are allowing students to call teachers by their first names, this is very unusual and, in my view, ill-advised. In most cases a young gentleman precedes his teacher's surname with Mr., Mrs., Miss or Ms. A young gentleman treats every member of the administration—from the principal to the cafeteria workers—with the utmost respect.

A young gentleman does nothing to disturb the teacher's study plan or other members of his class. He completes his assignments from the evening before and is prepared every morning with the necessary school supplies. He sits in his seat only and does not invade the physical space of his classmates or take any of their supplies without permission. He does not chatter while the teacher is teaching or while others are working. He never copies from a classmate's paper.

In the cafeteria he remembers his table manners and does not take food from another child or make unkind remarks about another child's food or eating habits. He never throws food, and cleans up after himself in the instructed fashion.

On the playground a young gentleman waits his turn for swings and hanging bars and follows rules of play in whatever game is being played. He stops his play when recess is over and does not cause unnecessary stress for his supervisor by lagging behind.

A young gentleman does not wear a cap or hat in school, nor does he dress in ways that are not in compliance with a dress code. The practice of shagging—allowing pants to slip well below the waistline so that one's underwear is visible—is not allowed in most schools and is considered offensive to many.

YOU KNOW YOU ARE RAISING A GENTLEMAN IF . . .

He dresses in the fashion of the church he is attending; if jeans are acceptable apparel, he may wear them.

———

He adheres to the dress code of the school he is attending.

———

He does not chew gum in school or church.

———

He does not eat or drink in church.

———

He does not talk out of turn at school.

———

He does not make fun of a classmate's answer to a teacher's question, or the classmate's inability to answer a question.

———

He does not make fun of a classmate's grades on a test or report card.

———

When he needs to go to the rest room during church or temple, he does not disturb others on his route.

———

He does not wear a hat or cap in church, but wears a yarmulke into a synagogue, even if he is visiting and is not of the Jewish faith.

———

He addresses clergy and school staff by the appropriate titles.

———

He keeps his own place standing in line, never cutting in, and not pushing those ahead of him or holding up those behind.

———

Parent Pointers

Do not impose unruly children
on fellow congregants.

――――

Supply small boys with something to
occupy them during the service. Do not
supply your child with toys and diversions
that will disturb others.

――――

Dress appropriately for church.
Hats for women are fine; hats for men—
other than yarmulkes—are not.

――――

Do not whisper, chit-chat, or giggle
with your spouse, friends, or children
during the service.

――――

Pay attention to the service,
including the sermon, and do not use the
time as an opportunity to pay bills or
catch up on correspondence.

――――

Encourage your son to participate in the
service when he is old enough.

―――

Address the clergy
with their proper titles.

―――

Get your children to school on time,
properly dressed, and prepared with what
they need for the day.

―――

Do not express disrespect for the
teacher or administrator to your children
or in front of your children.

―――

Let your children know
that in the school the faculty and
administration are in charge.

―――

If there is a disagreement
between your child and a teacher or an
administrator, address it privately with the
appropriate school representatives.

Try This At Home

At many churches that hold more than one service on Sundays, one is typically more family-friendly—usually it is the early service. Getting young children ready for church on Sunday mornings can be frantic, and what gets left behind is something to keep them occupied, which is why you see so many mothers digging through their purses looking for pen and paper on which her child can draw. Keep some things that are appropriate for church in your car: a sketch pad, a coloring book, and a plastic bag full of crayons (*not* a pencil box, which can get very loud when kids rattle it around looking for a particular color), a work book, or a favorite picture book. These also come in handy at restaurants that do not distribute kiddie diversions.

Some Good Advice

Everyone is busy, pressed for time, under-helped, and overwhelmed. But make time—somehow, somewhere—to volunteer at your child's school. You will discover that there are endless opportunities, from weekly tutoring sessions to helping in the office or school clinic once every two weeks to chaperoning field trips a few times a year. It is the best way to get to know the teachers and school administration, as well as your child's friends and other parents. If they know you on a personal level, it can benefit your child. Even one hour a month makes a difference. Your child will be proud to have you there, so enjoy it while you can. Once he enters adolescence, if you dare to show up at his school, he will act as though he has never seen you before in his life.

Chapter Seventeen

GOOD SPORTSMANSHIP

Some of the most blatant exhibitions of bad sportsmanship ever witnessed have taken place not in professional sports stadium and arenas, but at children's soccer, basketball, hockey, softball, and baseball games. Even worse, the ugly outbursts have come, not from children, but from their parents. The most horrifying incidents make the national news, but even the most level-headed parents can get carried away in the heat of the moment and do shameful things. They may not beat up another father, but they may yell at an umpire who called their son out.

When my son was seven years old, he was playing a game in a YMCA basketball league on one side of the gym while two other teams played on the other side. My son's team finished early, and we stayed to watch the other match. We saw more than basketball. Immediately following the game, the mother of a player on the losing side walked briskly across the court to the coach of the winning team and slapped him hard across the face, she then grabbed her son's hand and walked out the door. You could have heard a jaw drop in that gymnasium; everyone— players, parents, referees—-was stunned into utter silence. Her own child was mortified, the coach was astounded, and the other parents and children were horrified. We all knew her to be a good mother. She was a devoted volunteer at the school and in the community. She was one of *us*, and it made us all feel a little bit ashamed.

Sadly, the son withdrew from the league; whether it was his choice or his mother's we don't know. The upside of this was that it challenged every parent there that day to take a good look in the mirror and reinforce the lessons of good sportsmanship.

Long before your son sets foot on a soccer

field or basketball court, he will have many
opportunities to learn good sportsmanship.
When playing board games, for instance, your
son will no doubt be disappointed if he is sent
to jail without passing go or sent back to
Gumdrop Village from the summit of Candy
Mountain. When your son experiences such a
setback do not be tempted to allow him to draw
again for a better card. The only way a child
can learn to be a good loser is by losing, seeing
that it is not the end of the world and that
earned success is all that much sweeter.

My son is an excellent athlete, but it pains
me to say that the art of being a good loser has
with some difficulty. His superior motor skills,
competitiveness, and perfectionism combine for
some potentially volatile moments on the
playing field. It has not been a lesson easily
learned, requiring repeated drills, reminders,
positive reinforcement, and tough love,
including pulling him out of a game or off a
field when his conduct warrants it. But, good

sportsmanship is an essential character tool for every young man, and for those who are athletically inclined, it is as important as being able to pitch a baseball or score a goal.

Once your son is signed up for a team sport, you relinquish authority to the coach when he is on the field or court. When playing in a team sport, a young gentleman acknowledges his coach's authority and role and relinquishes his individual aspirations for the common goal of the team.

A coach is charged with teaching the rules of the game and good manners during the competition. Besides a strong pitching arm, or quick feet, there are more intangible tools a young man brings to the game. A young gentleman has a positive, generous attitude, always aware that a team sport requires teamwork. He doesn't hog the ball but passes to a teammate who is in a better position to score. If he misses the shot or strikes out, he can show that he is disappointed, but he does not stomp his feet, kick the goal post, throw the bat, or toss his batting helmet. In some sports, unseemly shows of temper are enough to get a player ejected from the game. I have always found the penalty box in hockey to be a good compromise. In the heat of competition misconduct will occur, but making the offending player sit in the penalty box allows for different degrees of punishment: one minute, two minutes, or more. We have occasionally employed the penalty box concept at home for behavior infractions. The fighting that is common in hockey is never condonable, and people who cheer it on at hockey games share in the dishonor of the pugilists.

A young gentleman doesn't question or argue the decisions of the coach or the call of the umpire or referee, nor does he roll his eyes or make disrespectful faces. When it is time for the sides to change, or play to resume, he hustles and does not hold up the game. A young gentleman does not offer excuses for a mistake or bad play—the sun was in my eyes, I had a crick in my neck—but apologizes to his teammates for any lapse that may have hurt the team. A young gentleman accepts the apology from a teammate who made and error, and he does not make fun of an error of a member of the opposing team.

In most children's sports, after the game is concluded, both sides line up and shake hands— or exchange hand slaps—with the opposing players. A young gentleman participates in this ritual with sincerity, without grumpiness or boasting, remembering that being a gracious winner is as important as being a good loser.

The rules of good sportsmanship apply to any competition, whether it is organized sports or playground kickball, a casual race across the swimming pool or a crucial swim meet, or a friendly game of Monopoly. Be fair, be generous, be accommodating, be flexible, and be willing to compromise. Without those principles of play, no one wins.

You Know You
Are Raising A Gentleman If . . .

He does not gloat over a win
or sulk over a loss.

———

He does not accuse another player of
cheating, even if he knows it to be true.

———

He knows the rules of play but is
willing to consult the rule book if a
call or play is in dispute.

———

He yields to the authority of his
coach and referees.

———

He does not cross the line between
aggressive play and assault.

———

He does not deliberately harm, push, pull,
or elbow another player, despite what he
may see on television.

———

Good Sportsmanship

He stays engaged in the game,
on the field or on the bench.

_____

He does not make fun of another player's
mistakes, even players on opposing teams.

_____

He commends the efforts of a teammate,
even if that effort fails.

_____

He acts as a booster for his teammates.

_____

He congratulates the winner if he
loses and thanks the losers for a good
game if he wins.

PARENT POINTERS

Do not let your children win a game.

_____

Remind your son that games are
meant to be fun, and if his conduct is
making it less so, he cannot play.

_____

Remind your son to include everyone
who wants to play in the game, even if the
child's ability is not commensurate
with his teammates.

———

Help your son learn the rules and peculiar
courtesies of the game or sport in which
he has chosen to participate.

———

Yield to the authority of the coaches and
referees. If they need your advice,
opinion, or help, they will ask.

———

Do not do anything to embarrass your
child, whether that be cursing at the
umpire or calling your son by a private
family nickname when he comes to bat.

———

Resist the urge—this is particularly true for
mothers—to run onto the field or court
and check your child's injury.

———

Resist the urge—this is particularly true for fathers—to usurp the coach's game plan or question his decisions.

_____

If you have a question about a decision or your son's playing time, consult privately, calmly, and non-confrontationally with the coach after the game.

_____

Never berate, yell, or curse at your son, his teammates, opposing players, opposing coaches, opposing parents, or officials.

_____

Act as every child's booster, not just your own. This includes commending a particularly exceptional play by an opposing player.

_____

Congratulate the winners if you lose; commend the losers for a good effort if you win.

Try This At Home

I absolutely abhor the playground practice of "picking" teams; one by one, the best players are chosen, as the lesser ones shrink slowly, inch by inch, into the earth, until finally, only two remain, thoroughly humiliated, dreading the next selection that will reveal which of the two is the *least* wanted child. I am not an advocate of finding every inane opportunity to boost a child's self-esteem, but this practice destroys a boy's confidence. Parents, teachers, and PE instructors should make sure they use a less discriminatory way. For example, place the children in a straight line and have them count off 1, 2, 3, 4, 1, 2, 3, 4. All the ones and threes go on one side, and all the twos and fours go on the other. Allowing children to "pick" the best players first in order to stack a team belies the lesson that it's just a game.

Some Good Advice

Often, a young boy is so disappointed in his play, or his failure, or the result of the game, that he will cry; in extreme cases, I have seen entire teams melt down. Competitions—ball games or spelling bees—are intense, and emotions are close to the surface. Crying is a better reaction to disappointment than anger or violence, and it is not a release permitted only to girls. Let a boy work through it and pull himself together; it only takes a minute. A good coach will pull the boy or boys aside for a moment, remind him that it is only a game, and say something to boost his self-confidence. As instinctual as it is for a parent to want to comfort his or her son, do not call attention to his crying by trying to console him yourself or by hissing at him to stop being a crybaby. A ten-year-old chess whiz or eight-year-old swimming star is still a child, not a miniature adult.

Chapter Eighteen

WRITTEN CORRESPONDENCE

Somewhere—in a special box, in his baby book, in the bottom of a drawer—are tucked away your child's first scribble-scrabbled communications. Short and sweet, embellished with a heart or a flower or a stick figure, they are infinitely endearing in their earnest simplicity.

Written correspondence is one of the greatest, most enduring and priceless gifts we can offer one another. There is a solid argument to be made for the marvels of e-mail and how well it facilitates easy and frequent communication among people who haven't put pen to paper in years. Yet there is still something very special about finding—amid the bills, advertisements, solicitations, appointment reminders, and credit card offers—a handwritten note or letter from an old friend, a faraway relative, or a favorite child.

According to standard rules of etiquette, there are three types of letters that should always be handwritten (unless a disability prevents it): notes of condolence; replies to formal invitations; and thank-you notes.

Children will have rare occasion to write condolence notes or formal invitations, but many more opportunities to write thank-you notes. Getting children into the habit of writing thank-you notes at an early age, even before they are able to write, is a good policy that will help them down the road. Make it fun for them, and make good use of their imagination. When my children were toddlers we used finger paints to put their handprints on sheets of paper, then they wrote their names as best they could. I would add a short note of my own. Later we graduated to drawing pictures of the gifts they had received, and finally worked our way up to writing. Stationery companies make pre-printed fill-in-the-blank thank-you cards for children.

"Dear _____, Thank you for the _____. I love it! _____" Frankly, I'd prefer a paper towel with a Kool-aid stain and a crayoned scrawl.

What is important is that your son understand that when someone is thoughtful enough to remember him with a gift that gesture must be acknowledged in a personal and prompt fashion (though late is better than never at all).

My son, as wonderful and generous and kind as he is, balks when informed that it is time to write thank-you notes. He would much rather be outside playing ball. Yours may do the same. I tell him quite simply that if he would prefer and if it would save him the time, I would be happy to spare him the trouble and send all of his gifts back. That is all the inspiration he needs to sit down at the table. While strict guidelines of etiquette call for thank-you notes for birthday gifts to be sent within two or three days of their receipt, we wait and do them all at one time.

A child's thank-you notes can be written on almost anything at all but providing a box of stationery that he chooses himself seems to make the endeavor more enjoyable. Additionally, children's stationery is usually ruled, which is helpful, and can be imprinted with your child's first name, making it more special.

More than any other type of letter, thank-you notes can be written in a conversational style, which is the way most children naturally write anyway. A young gentleman begins his thank-you note with the appropriate salutation: "Dear Grandma," "Dear Aunt Donnie," or "Dear Andrew." If the gift is from a family he writes, "Dear Frenches."

He acknowledges the specific gift with a brief note of what makes it special: "Thank you for the bat. I hit at least a hundred balls with it at the park yesterday!" or "Thank you for the *Red Wall* book. Those are my favorites and I am already on chapter four."

Boys' birthday parties are typically frenetic

affairs, but it is important that, when a young gentleman opens his presents, he keeps the accompanying card with the present or opens them at a slow pace, allowing someone to keep a list of the gifts and the givers. It is rude to race through a pile of presents.

If he received cash, he makes some mention of how he has used it, or intends to. "Thank you for the check for $25. I used it to get a new game for my Game Boy." Or, "Thank you for the check for my birthday. My mom is taking me to Borders Books to look for something special." In the case of a gift certificate, he can write, "Thank you for the gift certificate to the Games Store. They have the coolest things and I can't wait to go!"

If the gift is from a friend who came to a birthday party, he might add, "Thanks for coming to my party. It was fun." If the gift is from a relative who lives far away, he might say, "It was nice of you to remember me on my birthday. I wish you could have been here."

In closing, he can simply say, to a friend, "Thanks again. Harry." To a relative he could say, "Thank you again. Love, Harry." To someone far away, he can write, "I hope to see you soon. Harry."

A young gentleman who has fairly legible handwriting addresses the envelopes, then seals and stamps them, saving his parent the trouble.

When a boy is nine or ten years old, he is old enough to write and send the invitations to his own birthday parties. These can be pre-printed or designed by the young man on a computer if he has access to one.

You Know You Are Raising A Gentleman If . . .

He handwrites his thank-you notes.

———

He acknowledges a gift with a thank-you note as promptly as possible.

———

He includes a reference to the specific gift in the thank-you note; he does not say, "Thank you for the birthday present."

―――――

He sends a thank-you note if he has been someone's guest on a special vacation or outing.

―――――

He never sends prank letters via the postal system or over the Internet.

―――――

He understands privacy issues when it comes to mail, via the postal service or the Internet, and never opens or reads another person's mail.

PARENT POINTERS

Handwrite your thank-you notes in a timely and personal fashion.

―――――

Get your son in the habit of writing
thank-you notes as young as possible; if he
can pick up a crayon, he is ready.

———

Allow your son to choose a box
of his own stationery and give him
a supply of his own return address
labels and stamps.

———

If he is too young to do so,
address the envelopes for him as
soon as he completes the letter.

———

Take your son to the post office or
mailbox to drop his letters.

Try This At Home

Another year, another birthday party, another
dozen toys to add to the pile in his bedroom or
playroom. When a major gift-receiving occasion
occurs, take the opportunity to cull from his
collection those toys or gadgets he no longer

plays with or uses. The toys he discards do not need to equal the number of gifts he has received, but should be significant. If the toys he is eliminating are in good condition, take them to a family shelter or day care center for indigent families.

SOME GOOD ADVICE

If you have Internet access, be aware of the dangers. Familiarize yourself with Internet filtering services that can block "adult" sites from your computer.

There are chat rooms specifically targeted for children, but that doesn't stop the thirty-eight-year-old pedophile in Kansas City from logging on as eleven-year-old Jimmy and chatting with your child. You may set up an e-mail address for your child on your computer with specific rules of engagement. There is an element of trust involved here; you would not open and read their mail delivered by the post office, and e-mails should be treated with the same privacy.

What you might do is make a list of approved friends with whom your son may communicate with via e-mail, along with their addresses. If you see unfamiliar names and addresses in your family computer e-mail box, you can ask your son who they are and decide if they should be added to his list of approved correspondents.

Most often your son will be e-mailing other boys or girls he has seen just one hour before at school. If your son has a friend who has moved to another city, e-mail can make keeping in touch easier. You might also consider, to save on long-distance phone bills, allowing them to use Instant Messaging—ultra-fast e-mailing between just two people that resembles an electronic conversation—if it is a service on your provider. They might pre-arrange a time on the computer once every two weeks when they would Instant Message one another.

Chapter Nineteen

GIVING AND RECEIVING

Every December since I was seven years old, I have hung the same special ornament on my Christmas tree. It began its holiday decorating career as a red Christmas ball, onto which had been glued a pair of blue eyes, a nose and a bow-shaped mouth; a little felt Santa hat with a piece of holly was perched on top, and from under the hat hung two braids of yellow yarn.

Until I left home it was stored with all of our other family ornaments, but it was never unwrapped or hung up by anyone but me. When I left at nineteen to move to New York City, along with my clothes, furniture, family photos, books, records, and diaries, I took the ornament, wrapped in tissue paper in a small box. That first lonely Christmas there in my dinky studio apartment, it was the only decoration I placed on my tabletop tree. My collection of ornaments grows larger every year, but that one started it all. It moved with me to six different apartments in New York then to Nashville and three different homes there. Over the years she cracked from one side to another, and I taped her back up again. Then she lost one eye, then her nose, and finally, the ball itself became so shattered, it was not repairable. The only parts that now remain on the hook are the hat and the braids, and they are looking pretty shabby, too. A couple of years ago, my children were laughing at the raggedy thing and asked me why I didn't just throw it away. Here is what I told them:

> When I was seven years old, my Brownie
> troop celebrated Christmas by making
> stockings of personal items and taking them to
> a nursing home for senior citizens, where we
> sang Christmas carols and had punch and
> cookies. Afterwards, we returned to the church

where we held our meetings for the eagerly awaited gift exchange. Every Brownie had been told to bring a gift with a three dollar limit. The wrapped presents were put in a pile, and one by one, we chose one and opened it. I was the last to pick, and watched as the other Brownies opened boxes of colored pencils, a game, or small pieces of jewelry. Finally, it was my turn and I opened the last small box. Inside was the ornament. I was sorely disappointed at such a useless gift, and if the look on my face wasn't obvious enough, I saw fit to say aloud, "What *is* this?" with a tone of utter dismay.

As soon as the words left my mouth, I knew I had done something really, really wrong. The little girl who had contributed the ornament— which she had made with her mother—-burst into tears. My ignominy was heightened by the fact that my mother was the Brownie leader. She was astounded at the behavior from her very own child, and she snatched me up from my seat so quickly I thought she

would pull my arm out of its socket. She
marched me out of the room and into the hall,
where she told me in no uncertain terms that
she had never been so embarrassed, or so
ashamed of me. Of course I had to apologize
to my fellow Brownie, and to her mother when
she came to pick up her daughter. For the rest
of the year, that Brownie didn't speak to me,
and I didn't blame her a bit. The odd thing
was that my reaction was completely out of
character for me, heretofore a warmhearted
and sweet-natured child, and to this day I still
have no idea what could have come over me
to treat another person so cruelly.

When we got home, I was sent to my room,
where I flung myself on my bed and cried and
cried. Finally, my mother came in and, now
somewhat calmed down, gave me a lecture on
kindness, decency, consideration, and respect,
but it wasn't really necessary; my friend's hurt
face that afternoon spoke volumes and had
already taught me all I needed to know. I wrote